Final Analysis

*A Decade of Commentary
on the Church and
World Missions*

Jim Reapsome

a division of the
BILLY GRAHAM CENTER
Wheaton College, Wheaton, IL 60187

Published by Evangelism and Missions Information Service,
a division of the Billy Graham Center,
Wheaton College
P.O. Box 794, Wheaton, IL 60189
630.752.7158

The Evangelism and Missions Information Service (EMIS) publishes *Evangelical Missions Quarterly* and *Pulse* newsletter. The purpose of EMIS is to inform, motivate, and equip missionaries and to help shape the theories, values, and practices of the evangelical missionary enterprise.

Other EMIS publications include:
Overcoming Missionary Stress, by Dr. Marjory Foyle
Conflict or Connection: Interpersonal Relationships in Cross-cultural Settings, by Levi Keidel
Don't Pig Out on Junk Food, by Alma Daugherty Gordon
The Directory of Schools and Professors of Mission and Evangelism, John Siewert and Dotsey Welliver, editors

For further information, write: EMIS, P.O. Box 794, Wheaton, IL 60189.

Printed in the United States of America

What others
have to say. . .

"Jim's words challenge my thinking, round out my perspective of God's work in the world, and stimulate my dreams for a speedier evangelization of the world. This book of 100 'Final Analysis' columns from Jim Reapsome's pen is a special treasure, as is its author to the missions community."
>—*John H. Orme*, *Executive Director*
>*IFMA, Wheaton, Ill.*

"Jim has the insight to discern what is otherwise obscure, the skill to articulate it well, and the grace and earned credibility to make us glad to read his words even when they hurt."
>—*Jim Plueddemann*, *General Director*
>*SIM International, Fort Mill, S.C.*

"Neither sentimentalist nor cynic, Jim Reapsome exemplifies the best in Christian journalism. He tells it like it is—and like it should be."
>—*Stan Guthrie*, *Editor of* World Pulse *and Managing Editor of* Evangelical Missions Quarterly
>*Wheaton, Ill.*

". . . Jim Reapsome brings us truths that are timeless and yet still as timely as today's headlines. As a seasoned interpreter of both the Word and the world scene, Jim skillfully fuses these two horizons. With perceptive passion he calls us to an informed response to both."
>—*John Gration*, *Professor of Missions Emeritus*
>*Wheaton College Graduate School, Wheaton, Ill.*

"His columns are easy to read and filled with biblical wisdom and practical insight."
>—*Ron Blue*, *President*
>*CAM International, Dallas, Tex.*

"I think of him as a brother whose gift is to 'provoke' (KJV) us to 'outbursts of love and good deeds' (NLT)."

—**Spencer Bower**, *General Director*
Christian Service Fellowship, Rogers, Minn.

"For decades Jim Reapsome has been a formative influence in evangelical missions. . . . So much of missiological writing is predictable, but not Jim Reapsome's."

—**Robertson McQuilkin**, *President Emeritus*
Columbia International University, Columbia, S.C.

"Jim is a faithful foot soldier of the kingdom who is not afraid to tell others of any rank how he thinks the Battle is going. These articles are his reports from the front lines."

—**Paul Borthwick**, *Senior Consultant*
Development Associates International, Lexington, Mass.

"Jim's homilies . . . have personalized and sensitized readers to the contemporary issues in global evangelizing and church growing. Pastors worldwide, church mission committees, students, missionaries and their lay supporters have understood more clearly the issues in world missions because of Jim Reapsome. . . ."

—**Will Norton, Sr.**, *Distinguished Professor of Missions*
Reformed Theological Seminary, Charlotte, N.C.

"Our missionary staff has greatly benefited from his gems over the years. His lessons are personal, practical, and premier."

—**Susan Perlman**, *First Assistant to Executive Director*
Jews for Jesus, San Francisco, Calif.

"Jim Reapsome has earned the right to be heard. A writer can have no greater praise. The missionary world of our day is indebted to him in ways many of us will never know."

—**Glenn Schwartz**, *Executive Director*
World Mission Associates, Lancaster, Pa.

"I suspect I'm one of many who turn immediately to Jim Reapsome's 'Final Analysis' column when each issue of *Pulse* arrives! Having his insightful and cogent articles on key missions issues brought together in this book will preserve them to bless future generations of missions leaders."

—**Bill Waldrop**, *Retired President ACMC; Facilitator of International Ministries Mission America, Colorado Springs, Colo.*

"Jim's column brings penetrating, sometimes painful, insights to bear on every stream of the missions community. Decades of experience observing the missions scene provide the balance—and the fuel—for his commentaries. Clearly, Jim loves the cause of world missions and its Lord enough to hold us to the high standards of Christ and his kingdom."

—**Sharon Mumper**, *Eastern European Magazine Training Institute, Baden, Austria, and former managing editor of* EMQ *and* World Pulse.

"Jim's fresh perspectives about the world of missions are always worth the price of a subscription. . . . His lifetime of walking in the sandals of missionaries—theorists and practitioners—has given him a credibility that makes his commentary on the current missions scene eminently worth mulling over. . . . He looks beyond the whats and the how manys to the whys and therefores. He always challenges us and often changes us."

—**Terry C. Hulbert**, *Professor, Columbia International University, Columbia, S.C.*

"Sometimes he's in your face. Other times, he sneaks up on you. . . . Whether challenging stale patterns, highlighting neglected truths, or blazing new trails, Jim has clarified my thinking as well as energized me to act more creatively and responsibly as a world Christian."

—**Kenneth Mulholland**, *President Evangelical Missiological Society, Columbia, S.C.*

"He has a unique ability to take current events, sporting events, and even a cereal bowl and come up with a biblical missions application. . . . Jim's parables have mentored me and many others over the years."

—*Tom Telford*, *Vice President of Mobilization*
United World Mission, Lederach, Pa.

"His ability to really see what is happening in world mission and his gentle reminders that mission is all about Jesus Christ . . . make 'Final Analysis' a must read."

—*Glenn O'Shoney*, *Executive Director*
Lutheran Church—Missouri Synod World Mission
St. Louis, Mo.

"I always learn from the style and substance of what Jim Reapsome writes. He gives us a lot to think about, and it doesn't always make us comfortable."

—*Gerald H. Anderson*, *Editor,* International Bulletin of Missionary Research *and Director of the Overseas Ministries Study Center, New Haven, Conn.*

"Missionaries all over the world have benefited from his salient and lucid writing. His authenticity stands up under close inspection. Jim is the real thing."

—*Gary Brumbelow*, *General Director*
InterAct Ministries, Boring, Ore.

"In 47 years of mission work nothing has been more valuable in keeping me up to date than the writings of my good friend Jim Reapsome. When *World Pulse* arrives, I turn immediately to 'Final Analysis.' Jim's keen insights, his lively and readable style, and his courageous challenges to mission leaders combine to make his writings enjoyable and indispensable. I am delighted to see his best columns put together for posterity."

—*David Howard*, *Special Assistant to the President,*
Cook Communications Ministries International,
Colorado Springs, Colo.

Contents

The Task Force

The Home Front

The Resources

The Cultural Challenge

The Obstacles

Foreword

The first time I ate oysters I sat opposite Jim Reapsome in a restaurant called Irelands, just north of the Loop in Chicago. He seemed so urbane, so experienced, a man of the world. After all, he knew about eating oysters. And he must have been all of 35 years old.

He had been offered a job editing a prestigious publication, and he had come to seek counsel from the editor for whom I worked. They dragged me along to make it a threesome. Something about the man struck me at that meeting. He was enjoying the life God had given him on earth, and at the same time he was focused. He had purpose, but he wasn't so single-minded he couldn't enjoy oysters. Serving God was serious business to him, but the fruits of the earth were gifts God had given him to savor.

That was close to 40 years ago. We have crossed paths as colleagues many times over the years, and I have grown to respect him more. His writing is a reflection of his heart and mind and personality. To read him is to get to know him—and appreciate him. For over a decade now he has watched and pondered the passing missions scene and pronounced judgment on it in his column, "Final Analysis." This book includes the best of those columns.

All that's very nice, and Jim's a fine man, but how can he enlighten us on the challenge of world missions at the beginning of a new millennium? He does it primarily as a journalist in the best sense of the word, who is both observer and reporter of the world around him. The tight, no-nonsense writing he learned on the newspaper serves him and us well, but it is much more than writing style that makes these observations valuable. It is Jim's sharp eye, the wisdom of experience, and his down-to-earth practicality—what my dad used to call old-fashioned horse sense—that makes me want to read what he writes.

Like every good journalist, Jim is an entertaining storyteller. He is plain-speaking, with a wry sense a humor, and, what I appreciate especially in our culture of hype—he doesn't take himself too seriously.

The good journalist has a critical eye, questioning all, not accepting anything at face value, asking why and how and when and where, and Jim has that. He leans against the culture, challenging, for example, the use of buzz words such as "contextualization" or doubting the wisdom of our faith in photography as the great means of communicating.

Only in recent years as I have visited various mission fields and talked to mission leaders have I realized how much his opinions and his leadership are valued. His name has come up in meetings in Singapore, Atlanta, Bangkok, and Chicago. The Evangelical Press Association made him an honorary member. His ministry has extended far beyond his computer.

I don't remember too much now about that lunch at Irelands. (After all, it was almost a career ago. Were the oysters fried, baked, on the half shell?) But looking back I'm thankful for that beginning of a friendship with a man whose quiet impact on missions and journalism will be fully appreciated only in the world to come.

Ron Wilson

Ron Wilson is senior writer/editor for OMF International (Littleton, Colo.) and executive director of the Evangelical Press Association (Charlottesville, Va.).

Introduction

My "Final Analysis" column was never intended to be the last word. The field of world missions is so fertile that we need the contributions of everyone. We are members of Christ's body, so we are responsible to serve one another with the gifts God has given us.

My gift seems to be missionary journalism. God got me started as a newspaperman. Later on I became the editor of a weekly Christian newspaper, *The Sunday School Times*, which devoted significant space to missionaries and mission agencies. Our directory of mission agencies was like the Good Housekeeping seal of approval. We were also fortunate to have people like Elisabeth Elliot and Bruce Olson writing for us.

My missionary education began with InterVarsity. Missionaries visited my campus and spoke at summer training camps. I was also significantly blessed and encouraged by a local church strongly committed to world missions. Then came the Urbana missionary conventions. I edited the 1957 convention book. That was an education.

Working for InterVarsity, I also visited and spoke at great missionary churches, from Park Street in Boston to Lake Avenue in Pasadena. The Lord also dropped me into many smaller churches in between.

But perhaps my greatest missionary education came from two sources—the various mission boards I was called to serve, and the editorial committee of *Evangelical Missions Quarterly*, which I helped to start in 1964. Some of those mission boards met monthly in the New York and Philadelphia areas. Having successfully negotiated the merger of a smaller board with a larger one, I went on to serve 22 years with that agency. There's nothing comparable to learning missions inside out. Visits to various fields overseas also greatly enhanced my knowledge and interest.

In the early days of the *Evangelical Missions Quarterly* every article had to be approved by the editorial committee. Hashing ideas back and forth for a full day with missionary heavyweights sometimes left me exhausted, but it never dampened my enthusiasm for producing the best possible reading for missionaries around the world.

Years later, when I was called to direct the Evangelical Missions Information Service (now the Evangelism and Missions Information Service) in Wheaton, publisher of the *Evangelical Missions Quarterly*, I inherited two newsletters, *Pulse* and *Missionary News Service*. In those days we brought out *Pulse* in regional editions. They included long, scholarly articles and reports of current events and trends in world missions.

After several transformations, we settled on *World Pulse* (one version), featuring shorter news articles and interviews. Then someone suggested I should write an editorial for the back page. I found sufficient editorializing in other fine periodicals, including those published by mission agencies. So I decided to scrap the traditional editorial approach.

First thing I wanted to do was grab the reader's attention with a story of some kind. Then gradually I tried to pull him or her along with a transition into my main point, or application to world missions. I also wanted to inject a bit of humor and use similes and metaphors. Most of all, I wanted to avoid boredom and pomposity.

Apart from style and approach, "Final Analysis" also had to find an audience. For whom was I writing? The readership of *World Pulse* is quite diverse, from mission board executives to Pennsylvania dairy farmers. Every member of ACMC gets a copy. *World Pulse* goes into seminary and Bible school libraries. It encircles the globe.

As you will see from the following 100 columns, my favorites from 1990 to 1999, the primary audience often is the local church—the missions committee, the pastor, and the faithful supporters of missionaries. Other times I write for missionaries. Often I try to bridge the gap, or build stronger partnerships between churches and their missionaries. Sometimes I write for people in mission agency management, or field leaders. In some cases, I speak to broad issues of theology, doctrine, and missiology. You will find examples of each in these pages.

A word about the structure of this book. You will note that I haven't tried to cover every possible aspect of missions. Instead, I have clustered columns on related subjects. This approach gives readers what I think is a well-rounded look at current issues. Some topics get a lot more ink than others. I make no claim to missiological exhaustiveness, but taken together, I believe the columns present a broad picture of issues the missions community faces.

The most frequent question I get is, "Where do you get your ideas?" My primary answer is, from God through prayer. I never write without praying. How does God give me ideas? Many ways. Reading and observation are critical. I try to look at everything through the lens of world missions. I comb through letters and e-mails. I listen to missionaries talk. I sit around the table with them. I read things that are not directly related to missions. Somehow, an idea strikes me.

I always look for interesting stories, either in current

events, or in history, or in my life. I get ideas walking through parks, sitting in restaurants, looking at films, and watching a fly crawl across a man's bald head. I pray for compelling ideas that will make a difference.

Writing just to fill space, or get a byline, is a waste of time. Words must make a difference. "Final Analysis" should make readers think, challenge assumptions, and ponder possible changes.

I have no illusions that my ideas are the best, or that my columns will solve all the problems in world missions. Many readers have written with better ideas and perspectives. Praise God. We must keep on looking for better ways to do what is most important to the Lord Jesus, winning people to him and building his church.

I thank God for the gift of writing. I thank him for the inestimable privilege of serving the world missions community, churches, and missionaries. I have had the grandest, most satisfying calling. My prayer is that this collection of "Final Analysis" columns will continue to honor God, to the praise of his glory in the Lord Jesus Christ.

Jim Reapsome
Wheaton, Ill.
July 5, 1999

ACKNOWLEDGMENTS
I wish to thank Ken Gill of the Billy Graham Center for his initiation and encouragement of this compilation of my columns; Stan Guthrie for his editing; Dona Diehl for her production and graphics work; and Jean Warren and Karen Rummel of the *World Pulse* staff for their valuable assistance. I want to thank my wife Martha for her faithful partnership in life and ministry and her helpful critiques. Thank you, also, to my friends and supporters from College Church in Wheaton, Ill., Congregational Bible Church in Marietta, Pa., and Calvary Church in Lancaster, Pa.—*JR*

The Task

An African curve ball

B ack in the 1970s the editors at *Christianity Today* **enjoyed loads of fun with their readers by planting fake ads in the classified section.** They were bizarre and outrageous, but they contained just enough truth to perform the valuable service of a self-inflicted critique on some of our evangelical foibles. But they had to drop them when a newspaper reporter took one of the ads literally to illustrate how crazy evangelicals really are.

I thought of that the other day when I saw a classified ad in *CT* put there by an African who wants to be a missionary to the United States. His ad throws a curve ball at our typical understanding of world missions. Assuming *CT* hasn't revived its old tricks, his appeal forced me to ask whether or not we can see missions as a two-way street. Are we willing to be receivers as well as senders?

When your aircraft is 19th in line for takeoff, you have only one thing in mind: go, go, go. That's the way it's been in world missions. The U.S. church is like a vast missionary airport, with planes (new missionaries) waiting for the control tower to clear them for takeoff (the long wait for support). But there's something strangely wrong with our airport: No planes are arriving. Everything in missions is outgoing because we have the power, the people, and the plans.

Oh, the people who receive our planes are wonderful. They provide runways for us, help us unload our baggage, teach us their language, and generally set up shop for us so we can do for them what we have already decided they need done for them. How gracious of them to stroke us, so we can be fulfilled in what we want to do for them.

But let one of them say, "I'd like to be a missionary to your country," and we sit up like professionally trained, experienced pilots and retort, "What? You can't fly a missionary aircraft. What courses have you passed to qualify? Besides, we don't have any runways for you. You don't fit our culture. We don't have a slot for African missionaries in the United States. We don't need you. Stay home and evangelize your own country."

How wonderful to keep on giving and never receiving, to keep on saying we are strong and you are weak, we have great churches and you don't, we have courses in Greek, theology, missiology, and anthropology, and you don't, we have years of expertise and you don't, we have lots of money and you don't.

How stupid to keep on denying what the Bible teaches about oneness in the body, to keep on denying that every part of the body needs all other parts, to keep on denying that people who receive our missionaries don't have anything to teach us, to keep on cheating our schools and our churches out of learning from brothers and sisters in the so-called weaker, younger churches.

We don't act this way unconsciously, but deliberately. We actually refuse to give our sisters and brothers from overseas time in our pulpits and classrooms. Our 60 minutes on Sunday morning are so programmed and so precious we don't even allow people representing our churches overseas five minutes to give us a report.

How painfully difficult it is to take the seat of a learner and sit at the feet of an African, an Asian, or a Latin American. How painful it is to admit that our sisters and brothers have learned more and better spiritual lessons than we have, that they can preach the Bible more powerfully than we can. We need them to teach and evangelize us.

If God is telling them to come here, that's a significant sign. Are we ready for them? I doubt it. I hope the African who put that ad in *CT* gets at least one invitation.

Bruce Olson's legacy

When Bruce Olson and his mule ventured into **Venezuela's uncharted jungles 33 years ago, ranchers drummed some common sense into him.** "There are tame Indians and wild Indians," they said, "so be sure you locate the former and not the latter." But having never seen one, he was in no position to judge.

He had gone to Caracas to prepare for his mission to the Indians, because while in high school he was convinced this was what God wanted him to do. While working for the government in the Ministry of Health and studying at the university, he saw the Motilones on God's compass.

One day in 1964 he came to our home with his jungle diary, and a couple of wicked looking Motilone spears. I published his diary and these spears graced our walls for years. Our kids loved Bruce and his stories gripped them. So much so that when our daughter got married she asked for the Motilone spears. Now they've gone to Santiago, Chile.

On his first jungle trek, Bruce wandered around in circles for hours, stopped for the night, discovered he had no machete, nor a tool to open his sardines. He sat down on the trail with his mule, and decided that since the mule wasn't scared, he would be all right. Doing what he did was like launching a space shot to the moon. But look at the record of what God has done since Bruce and his mule set out from Machiques in the foothills of the Andes.

The so-called "wild" Indians have been transformed by the Lord Jesus Christ. Bruce has seen the work of the Holy Spirit continue to the next generation of Motilones. But they not only have redemption and new life, they also have the technical preparation they need to survive on the lands of their forefathers. Their lands, by the way, are now protected legally, thanks in great measure to Bruce's tireless efforts on their behalf.

Tribal students are academic achievers—15 are studying in university, next year 13 will graduate from high school, 22 from vocational training, and 12 from the school of nursing. All of the 400-plus previous Indian graduates are serving their tribes in the jungle. Not one has abandoned the jungle for city life. In the jungles more than 2,500 students are getting bilingual education in 18 languages.

Bruce has built facilities and trained people to work in 18 health centers, 42 bilingual schools, 22 agricultural centers, and 11 trading posts, which really are co-operatives. They spark social development in places overlooked by the governments of Colombia and Venezuela. The co-ops provide the economic base for 18 tribal peoples.

The director of the Bureau of Indian Affairs for Northeast Colombia is a Motilone lawyer. The director of Indian Affairs for the state government is a Motilone graduate in business administration. The coordinator for press relations for Northeast Colombia Native People's Affairs is a Motilone university graduate in journalism.

How has all this come about? Obedience, faith, courage, suffering, wisdom, and persistence by a young, unheralded missionary who did not bring Jesus to the Motilones as a foreign import but as one who sojourned their "trails of life's experiences."

Today's missionaries, churches, and agencies should gorge on Bruce Olson's story like kids chomping on fresh-sliced watermelon. We need this story to reinforce our faith and to stir up the current crop of high school and college students. People in our churches need to know it because they are subjected to misleading propaganda about the failures of missionaries and how they have destroyed indigenous cultures. Bruce Olson's story is the best answer I know to people who gripe, "What's the point of sending missionaries?"

Capt. O'Grady's life line

A friend of mine who knows about such things tells me that the biggest battle in the churches today is over music and worship styles. I believe him, because I run into this question everywhere I go. We are not fighting so much about issues of theology and doctrine, but about praise choruses and traditional hymns. The devil is having a field day, because every such intramural fight is a gain for his schemes to keep us from doing our primary mission—breaking down the walls of his kingdom of darkness and rescuing people for God's kingdom of light.

Like the Marines who flew into Bosnia and plucked Capt. Scott O'Grady from danger, we engage in rescue missions. They did not sit around and argue about which arrangement of the Marine Corps hymn to sing.

They pursued a single mission—rescue a downed pilot—and they allowed nothing to sidetrack them.

When Christians fight each other over music, their energies evaporate into nothingness like a morning ground fog. I'd be foolish to try and settle the music and worship styles debate, but God is not pleased when we draw a line in the sand between choruses and hymns. So fractious and dispiriting is the argument that on one Bible college campus some of the students refused to sing hymns.

Capt. O'Grady's saga shipped me into a "back to the future" mode. Old hymns like "Throw Out the Life Line" and "Rescue the Perishing" flooded my mind. Actually, I could not remember the last time I had been in a church service where these old hymns were sung. Possibly many readers don't even know what hymns I'm talking about.

I don't belong to the hymn preservationist society, but I do belong to the theological truth preservationist society. Those old hymns never tickled my ears musically, and their style has been banished to the realms of the passenger pigeon. But I fear that along with tossing those hymns into the musicological dustbin we may also be discarding the theological truths they intoned. Not just the bare truths, but the passion undergirding them.

Could it be that our laid-back, somewhat cavalier attitude toward world mission is traceable to our failure to sing the truths of "Throw Out the Life Line" and "Rescue the Perishing"?

Our theological jugular vein has been cut and we are bleeding to death while we fight over music and worship styles. How many people picture their mission—and their church's—as graphically compelling as throwing a life preserver to a drowning person? How many Christians really see their neighbors near and far like drowning people?

Millions of Capt. O'Gradys languish in the throes of apparent hopelessness because no one cares enough to rescue them from Satan's clutches. The heroism and determination of the Marine pilots to rescue Capt. O'Grady should stir us from our complacency. We've got to get our priorities straight, whatever we sing and however we sing it. If we insist on worship styles that feed our own needs, and ignore the fate of those who have never heard of the Lord Jesus Christ, we are derelict and indictable before our heavenly judge.

Jesus will not ask us whether we sang from overhead transparencies or hymnals. He will not ask if we sang contemporary praise choruses or 19th century classics. As the old saying goes, we must keep the main thing the main thing, which is to throw life lines of hope and peace to people trampled and overcome by despair.

Our theology of world missions must never become so sophisticated and technological that we forget to throw out the life line of the gospel to rescue people perishing in their sins.

Church planting's forgotten sizzle

In the heyday of Evangelism-in-Depth some 30 years ago, I visited a Guatemalan Indian believer who told me a story about his persistence in personal work I've never forgotten. He did door-to-door witnessing in his village, but didn't quit after his initial visits. Typically, people slammed their doors in his face, but that did not deter him. One house in particular intrigued him and he went back time and again, suffering rebuff each time, but on his 25th visit the family opened the door and he brought them to faith in Christ.

I thought about that Indian brother when I noticed in the paper that before a broker can go to work for Edward D. Jones & Co., he must visit the homes of 1,200 prospective customers, introducing himself, explaining the Jones investment philosophy, and leaving his business card.

Both stories reminded me of the critical ingredient in church planting: persistent hard work. Which brings up a nagging fear of mine. Are we in danger of assuming that the people we are sending overseas to plant churches are skilled soul-winners?

I use the term "soul-winner" deliberately because it has been cast on the language junk heap like a rusted out '73 Ford. Another term suffering the same fate is "personal worker." We're too sophisticated now for those relics of fundamentalism, but what have we lost? We have diluted our basic missionary image and purpose, namely, witnessing to and winning people to Christ.

What has replaced those antiquated words? Church planting. I know the rationale behind the words. It's not enough to win souls, you have to gather them into churches and disciple them. Fair enough. But wait a minute. What do you think has happened to the converts made by missionaries over the last century? They are filling churches and serving Christ all over the globe. Those missionaries planted churches, not because they were church planters, but because they were personal workers, evangelists, and soul-winners.

Are we quibbling over words? Not at all. I'm afraid that in our zeal to send church planters overseas we are in danger of forgetting their prime requirement: They must know how to go back to slammed doors 25 times, they must know how to make 1,200 house calls and introduce people to Jesus.

When from our pulpits and in our literature we persistently sell the church planting missionary image, we dull the knife of personal evangelism and omit the first step. We sugarcoat it, if you please. We make it sound like an ecclesiastical process, not life-and-death, not pounding the pavement, not taking rebuffs and insults, not agonizing in prayer with our sweat and tears. Church planting is sound missiology; soul-winning pumps virility into it.

Church planting as a missionary role model sounds as sterile for growing good soul-winners as Love Canal is for growing tomatoes. It lacks sizzle. We have to recapture the burning fire behind evangelism and personal work when we promote and recruit for missions.

Would-be McDonald's franchisees have to pass a training program that can take up to three years. It starts with the basics of making hamburgers. Can we in world missions afford to do anything less? Where do our church planters learn how to "make hamburgers"?

God's paramedics

Broken bodies and shattered glass crashed across the TV screen, vivid, tragic evidence of the latest suicide bombing in Tel Aviv. Paramedics frantically hustled off the limp, bloody body of a little girl lying on a stretcher. "What are they doing, Granddaddy?" my 4-year-old granddaughter asked me.

"They're taking the little girl to the hospital."

"Why?"

"Someone threw a bomb into a restaurant," I said, "and a lot of people got hurt by flying glass."

"Why did they do that?"

I paused and thought hard. Glib answers eluded me. What could I say that would make sense to a 4-year-old? Finally, I said, "They were very angry. Sometimes people get so angry they do bad things."

Meanwhile my thoughts plunged ahead in a different direction. A house in Israel with a hole in the roof. A packed crowd of onlookers, but no sirens, no blood. Men carrying a helpless victim—not out of the house, but into it.

Suddenly, the whole scheme of God's mission flashed before me. Whether it was the paramedics carrying a wounded child to the ambulance, or the four men who tore a hole in a house roof to lower a helpless man into the presence of Jesus, they epitomized the church's part in God's mission. People of faith do everything in their power to connect hurting people with the source of healing.

Everyone can identify with victims of tragic explosions and debilitating illnesses. Jesus said this world is sick, sick unto death, because of the infection of sin.

Prophets and apostles alike preached powerful sermons about the horrible effects of sin. The world is bleeding to death.

Everyone can identify with physicians, surgeons, nurses, and hospitals. Most of us at one time or another have spent some time in a hospital. Jesus said he is our physician, surgeon, and nurse all in one. He is the only one who can heal us from the ravages of our sins.

We can identify with the countless helpers who wheel us in and out of X-ray rooms, operating theaters, and re-covery rooms. I remember well the paramedics who scraped me off an icy parking lot, stuffed me into an ambulance, and sped me off to the nearest hospital where it became clear that I had broken my hip in a nasty fall. Who plays the role of these helpers in God's mission?

In this three-act play on the world stage, paradoxi-cally, the former victims are supposed to become the helpers. Jesus Christ rescues, heals, and liberates us. He sets the victims free. How the erstwhile victims love to celebrate their redemption and forgiveness.

But that's just Act 1. We know the second act. Jesus has not retired to accept our applause. He still welcomes sinners. He still loves to declare, "Today salvation has come to this house."

But where are the players for Act 3? Where are the healed victims who are supposed to carry the people to Jesus? Where are the helpers in God's mission? Where is their faith? Their obedience? What are they doing with themselves since Jesus set them free? Have they not understood that they are supposed to live as free people enslaved to Christ?

God's mission for all of us is simply to carry the

wounded, bleeding, and dying to Jesus. Next time you watch the rescuers at work after a bomb blast, think of your part in God's mission and then decide to enlist as his helper. Jesus will show you what to do.

Living down imperialism

"Imperialist" is the world's worst epithet.** The West accused the Soviets and the Chinese of being imperialists, and vice-versa. Missionaries from the West have found that they cannot escape this inflammatory designation.

Like a huge oil spill fouling some pristine beach, the charge of imperialist sticks to everything missionaries do and creates a messy obstacle to a clear, simple, winsome gospel witness. Covered with tar as they are, missionaries often try to escape by naively denying the charge, without examining it more seriously.

Obviously, they can't be imperialists, because they have neither political nor economic power aspirations. That's the way missionaries see themselves, as completely above the world's power struggles.

Unfortunately, however, the unbelieving world, especially in places where oppression, poverty, hunger, and exploitation are at their worst, sees the Christian missionary as part and parcel of the West's overwhelming power. Why? Because missionaries come with power oozing from their pores like ketchup belching from a squeeze bottle.

Missionaries' accoutrements of power are awesome, beginning with the paycheck and extending to equipment and communications power and the ability to grant relief, whether food, medicine, or whatever. To some beleaguered tribal peasant or slum dweller, the missionary represents power, i.e., imperialism, far beyond anything he or she has ever seen, or most likely ever will see.

This power, from the missionary's viewpoint, is used for good: to communicate the gospel, to teach, to bring relief from suffering and so on. However, from the recipients' perspective, this good, well-intentioned missionary work looks like high-powered propaganda (they know the cost of radio and TV time and of printing). Money, goods, training, and jobs go to the poor who convert to Christianity. This looks like bribery.

Tribespeople are converted not only to Christianity, but to Western clothing, values, and mores. The old ways are treated rudely and soon wither. This looks like cultural imperialism.

Is this a no-win situation for missionaries? Are they damned to be imperialists whatever they do? Perhaps so. However, we must not pretend that this public perception doesn't matter. It matters a great deal. It has serious ramifications for the entire missionary enterprise, but especially for America's senders and goers.

Knowing we are perceived as imperialists ought to squelch our triumphalism, our offensive "we're No. 1" attitude that often propels us overseas. It ought to remind us that people out there are not "targets," but real flesh and blood human beings, suffering abominably, and who deserve not high-powered, impersonal "campaigns," but compassionate understanding and love.

Missions is not a bottom-line production to be run according to Western media models, or like a pro football team, or a bureaucratic charity. We have to learn to bring Jesus to people without either psychological or economic manipulation. We have to struggle to live down everything—even our good technology—that mitigates against our being perceived as humble servants of Jesus Christ and of the people he sends us to. The gospel must truly be free from all taint, or hint, of imperialism of any kind.

Michelangelo, and worse

Michelangelo Buonarroti (1475-1564) grabbed more headlines in the U.S. than he ever did in his native Italy because some wise PR guys named a computer virus after him. Never mind that the crisis generally evaporated as quickly as a salesman of bogus stock. The fear merchants succeeded in driving people to spend a lot of money to protect their hard drives. It was a case of what you can't see can hurt you real bad. "Where did this demon virus come from?" and "How can it worm its tentacles into my innocent PC comfortably ensconced in the privacy of my own home?" were the choice topics of conversation for a week or so before the projected crash date, March 6, 1992.

A lot of mission agencies could have been drastically affected, had Michelangelo managed to infect their donor records and mailing lists, for example. You're talking about the lifeline of missions here, not a minor glitch.

But are donor records and mailing lists, essential as they are, really the lifeline of missions? In one sense, yes. Without donors, whether individuals or churches, vast chunks of the whole enterprise would simply melt away like the frost before the morning sun.

But what other viruses lurk out there, ready to attack, weaken, and eventually paralyze world missions? What other, more vital, lifelines risk being demolished beyond the financial ones? Too often, it seems, we give the impression that money really is our only lifeline to the future. But let's think for a moment about some fates worse than a computer crash.

What about a virus that destroys our love for God himself, whom we are supposed to love with the totality of our being? Or one that incessantly chips away at our promise to follow Jesus Christ as Lord, no matter what? The one that devours our promise to be his disciples, even if it means cutting back on our spending and consumption so that the poor, the addicted, the broken, the depressed—the world of suffering, hopeless people— can be helped and taught about Jesus?

What about a theological terror on the loose, a virus that sneaks into our churches and undercuts the uniqueness of Christ and the gospel as the only hope for people and the only security for eternity? A virus that tantalizes us with the notion that, in the end, somehow all will be saved? A virus that encourages us to be tolerant rather than dogmatic, and allow as how all faiths are trying to accomplish the same thing?

What about the virus that coddles us into thinking that world missions is the hobby, and responsibility, of a few fanatics, but certainly doesn't have anything to do with all of us in the church? A virus that effectively blocks the total mobilization of the church to get serious about world evangelization? A virus that detours a single-minded determination to bend every effort to get the gospel out to the millions of people who have never once heard the name of Jesus?

What about the virus of conspicuous consumption of Christian resources—videos, music, tapes, books, seminars, retreats, conferences, camps, buildings, schools, and so on—in the West, while we treat the rest of the Christian world community like beggars? A virus that overloads our circuits with so many market-driven helps to spirituality?

Against all of these noncomputer viruses we are as helpless as a field mouse against a diving sparrow hawk. There's no PR campaign to alarm us about the coming doomsday. We can't buy a program to protect us against these insidious viruses, but all of them conspire to sever the lifeline of aggressive world missions.

Jesus talked much about the dangerous, seductive spiritual viruses rampant in his day. He constantly bombarded his disciples with warnings like, "Beware!" and "Watch out!" and "Be on your guard against . . .!" He clearly exposed the viruses and his disciples consistently missed his point. That's what frightens me. Do we really know the viruses that can cripple world missions? I hope so.

Rescue the captives

One of the magnificent late 19th century British military expeditions conquered no new lands for Queen Victoria. You won't find it mentioned in standard history books, but because of the monumental logistics, military historians compare the landing in Ethiopia in 1868 to the Allies' Invasion of France in 1944.

In 1868 Emperor Theodore III of Ethiopia held a group of 53 European captives (30 adults and 23 children), including some missionaries, in a remote, 9,000-foot high bastion deep in the interior. Among them were a British consul and a special diplomatic emissary sent to secure the release of the prisoners. By letter, Queen Victoria pleaded in vain with Theodore to release the captives. Finally, the government ordered a full-scale military expedition from India to march into Ethiopia—not to conquer the country and make it a British colony, but simply to rescue a tiny band of civilians who had suffered in prison for more than four years.

The invasion force included 32,000 men, heavy artillery, and 44 elephants to carry the big guns. Provisions included 50,000 tons of beef and pork and 30,000 gallons of rum. Engineers built landing piers, water treatment plants, a railroad, and telegraph line to the interior, plus many bridges. All of this to fight one decisive battle, after which the prisoners were released, and everyone packed up and went home.

The British expended millions of pounds to rescue a handful of captives. Today our world is packed with millions of people who need to be rescued. These captives need the rescue of Jesus described to Paul. "Open their eyes and turn them from darkness to light and from Satan's power to God," Jesus told him.

In some eras Christian rescues floundered and flickered. But somehow the gospel spread and captives by the millions were set free. Toward the end of the 19th century, and again after campaigns missionaries suffered incredible hardships and many of them died. From their faithful witness came a mighty stream of conversions and new churches so that today those mission fields have more Christians than we do at home.

Nevertheless, stubborn outposts of resistance still

hold millions of captives. Satan has not released his prisoners. The advancing church gains little ground here against the strongholds of darkness.

When I read about the enormous investment by the British to save 53 people in Ethiopia in 1868, it occurred to me that something like this might well be required in our generation's spiritual welfare. For some Christians, the fight to release the captives resembles a slight skirmish carried on by a few volunteers. They think it's the kind of campaign that can be carried on without seriously impinging on their lifestyle.

Emperor Theodore III stalled and toyed with his prisoners as long as he received nothing more serious than threatening letters. But when the British forces actually appeared at his gates—after a grueling 400-mile march from the sea to a 9,000-foot high plateau—the captives walked to the British lines.

Their expedition was courageous, tough, and very costly. To the British, the prize was worth the cost. When the church realizes that obedience to Jesus, and the lives of the prisoners, are worth the cost, Christians will mobilize rescue operations to bring their full power to bear on the fortresses of fear, desperation, and darkness. A Christian student from another country put it this way: "If your people were as interested in getting into my country as my people are in getting into yours, you would have no problem."

The body dump

Like red-hot branding irons, certain memorable photographs sear our souls. The little Vietnamese girl, set aflame by a blast of napalm, racing in terror down a village street. The brave Chinese student challenging a tank rumbling into Beijing's Tiananmen Square.

Last month another one smashed my psyche with all the subtlety of a Scud missile. Four colors. Front page of the *Chicago Tribune*. A bulldozer scraping up bodies of dead Rwandans like so much disposable rubble.

How many of the people who once lived in those crumpled bodies are now with Christ, which, the apostle Paul said, is "better by far"? How many entered eternity without him? Christians of a variety of churches and creeds were said to make up 80 percent of Rwanda's population.

The picture compels us to face the horrors of warfare, disease, and famine, and the world's rampant unfairness. There, but for God's grace, was I. Those Rwandan bodies also drive home a picture of what missionary work ought to be about—saving people for eternity with Christ. We too easily forget this, and fall into all kinds of well-intentioned roles which we label "missionary."

To people in the pews, missionaries are evangelists first. They take Christ to a lost world. That's the biblical priority, passion, and pattern. That dramatic photo told me that we must pour more of our people and money than we now do into aggressive evangelism, with sensitivity and compassion.

Of course, we also need other helpers, but it is appalling to see how much of our time, people, and money are expended on subsidiary operations. Ten years ago the

Mission Handbook reported what missionaries did. Thirty-three percent were planting churches, 29 percent were nurturing churches, and 38 percent were doing "other." In other words, two-thirds of all missionaries were not bringing people to Christ and gathering them into churches. Of reporting agencies, 9.3 percent listed church planting as a primary task, and 9 percent listed evangelism as a primary task. Only 15 percent of the boards cited evangelism as a general ministry category. Further proof that all of us need a powerful wake-up call to get back to the basics of preaching Christ and loving people to him. (Incidentally, the numbers are old because the *Mission Handbook* has not compiled them since then, but I have no solid evidence that they have changed significantly.)

It's time for a reality check. We must examine everything from top to bottom, to see if we really are winning lost souls to Christ and establishing churches.

How much of the other stuff should be jettisoned? How much of the things being done by the 85 percent of the agencies that don't do evangelism really qualify as "missionary" in the biblical sense? I'm not saying that missionary doctors, radio engineers, and pilots, for example, do not do useful things, but unless we are careful, evangelism will be swallowed up in the quicksand of support and maintenance functions. Besides, much of the support work could be done by capable people who are not missionaries.

When Hudson Taylor crisscrossed the United States and Canada, seeking prayers and volunteers for China's lost millions, he peppered his audiences with visions of lost souls. He compared China's daily death toll to the deluge of water pouring over Niagara Falls. His graphic picture gripped many Christians, motivating many to take the gospel to China.

Perhaps Zaire's dirty yellow bulldozer scooping up the bodies of dead Rwandan refugees will do the same for us. If that's to happen, however, our pastors and mission board leaders will have to hit our churches with something like Hudson Taylor's compelling zeal for the lost.

The parable of Flight 771

The captain of the Air New Zealand Boeing 767 faced a critical decision over the South Pacific as he headed for Auckland airport. Should he divert from his flight plan to find a tiny, single-engine lost Cessna? Over the protests of his crew, he decided to try to find the plane and guide it to safety.

What followed was an agonizing quest that forced me to use my TV's remote control more than I had ever done before. You see, NBC had decided to run "Mercy Mission: The Rescue of Flight 771" opposite "Monday Night Football" on ABC. On some Monday nights, the choice would have been easy, because not all pro football games are equally riveting, but this one pitted the Steelers against the Dolphins, and it was a dilly.

So, during those interminable commercial time-outs I clicked on Channel 5 to see how the pilots were coming along. While the pitchmen shilled beer, my stomach churned at the impossibility of the 767's finding the Cessna, which had lost some crucial navigational equipment. Fuel and daylight were rapidly consumed, making the likelihood of a rescue increasingly remote.

Somehow, the fate of 300-pound athletes pounding each other into the Miami turf did not seem as important as the life of a solitary pilot. They were playing a game, while courage and hope ebbed away in the cockpit of the Cessna. The Steelers scored again and I quit the game for good.

The Cessna's pilot had enough of the fruitless game of hide-and-seek in the clouds, so he pulled out his life jacket and prepared to give up and ditch his aircraft in the swelling ocean. But the captain of the 767 refused to allow him to do so. Persistently, with the tone and approach of a seeking father, he encouraged, cajoled, and bargained the lost pilot to keep on flying. Suddenly, there it was, the battered Cessna staggering along just above the waves. The lost was found! The pilot followed the 767's lights to a safe landing at rain-swept Auckland airport. Tears welled into my eyes. I don't do that during football games.

The lost was found. Luke 15. There it was. Jesus told stories about lost sheep, a lost coin, and a lost son. The captain of the 767 was the shepherd looking for his sheep, his son. The pilot of the Cessna was the whole world, helplessly, hopelessly lost, trying to find its bearings, but ready to quit and take a dive into the ocean we call eternity.

But what tore my heart out was the captain who kept his aircraft ceaselessly plunging into the clouds when he had every right to head for home. He could have said, "Sorry, old chap, we've given it our best shot and it just won't work." Instead, he kept on talking and flying at the same time. He refused to let the lost pilot go down.

Jesus is like that. Which means that those engaged in

world missions keep on going, trying to guide every lost soul to a safe landing, because God is in the clouds, as it were, ceaselessly looking for lost people. We go on mission not because it satisfies our needs, or swells our esteem, but because God flies on and on and on, rescuing people from ditching into eternity without him. That's his commitment. He sent Jesus on a mission that we are supposed to copy.

As I watched the captain bore holes in the clouds, scanning the sky for one insignificant Cessna, I saw Jesus on his mission for me. I saw missionaries pursuing the lost in gathering darkness. I saw them liberated from carrying the load of ultimate responsibility for finding people. In the clouds they can't even see what's going on, while God relentlessly, unerringly responds to distress signals. I saw a church that has no right to stay on its own flight plan, but rather is willing to be diverted into rough weather and uncharted skies for the sake of people all over the world who have no navigational signals to help them find God and eternal safety.

The taste of Coke

Ever since Coca Cola's president Robert Woodruff **said at the end of World War II, "In my generation it is my desire that everyone in the world have a taste of Coca-Cola" missionaries have been comparing Coke's "Great Commission" with their own.** Has everyone had a taste of Coke? Has everyone had a sip of the water of life, Jesus Christ, that quenches thirst eternally?

Coca-Cola knows pretty well how it's doing, and the

scorecard reads like an image of how well the church is doing. For example, U.S. consumption of drinks made by Coca-Cola (e.g., Coke, Diet Coke, Sprite, Fanta) far outpaces the rest of the world at 292 eight-ounce servings per person per year. In terms of resources (buildings, schools, radio and TV programs, camps, conferences, literature, money, staff people, and so on), the church in the U.S. is far ahead of churches in the rest of the world.

Coca-Cola knows very well how the rest of the world is doing: Brazil, 99 eight-ounce servings per person in 1990; Taiwan, 48; Turkey, 20; Indonesia, 4. Likewise, missions statisticians can tell us the numbers of Christians of various kinds around the world, and the places and ethnic groups that lack knowledge of the gospel.

You also find some striking dissimilarities. True, Coke has the advantage of being a single entity, compared to the church's rampant divisions, but nevertheless those churches and agencies committed to fulfilling Christ's Great Commission could very well pick up a few pointers from Coke's single-minded global passion.

Coke says, "We are increasingly global because 95 percent of the world's consumers are outside this country. It's that simple." Where are the world's lost people? Sure, they're all around us in the U.S., but if you're marketing the gospel in the good sense, you'll soon find that the bulk of your "consumers" (those who need Jesus) are jammed into places like Chad, Peru, Nepal, Mauritania, and Sri Lanka. When are our churches going to refocus according to a consuming global vision and passion?

Coke displays a long-term commitment to difficult markets. Our schools, churches, and mission agencies must make the same kind of commitment, refusing to back off because of either a lack of immediate response, or some political or religious opposition. In other words, staying power is demanded.

Coke brings foreigners into top-level management in Atlanta. Some missions leaders say this can't and shouldn't be done in their offices. Why not? We talk a good line and say world evangelization requires a total partnership, but so far it's been pretty much a one-way affair. The U.S. office pays the piper and calls the tune. It's time to get foreigners into the top missions jobs, too.

Coke exercises flexibility and boldness to expand its international business. Those two words ought to characterize our missions planning and operations, but somehow many churches and agencies seem stuck with a conservatism and caution that kill flexibility and boldness. It's as though changing the time-honored "Principles and Practices" of the mission is akin to rewriting the Ten Commandments. Religiously, politically, and economically the world is changing so rapidly that our churches and missions cannot afford to be inflexible and cautious. If there ever was a time to break out of the old ways of doing things, this is it.

Finally, says an outside analyst, Coke "can fill a package and put it on a shelf anywhere more efficiently than anyone." I would like to think that there are hundreds of young people and baby boomers who would jump at a challenge like that, for the sake of Jesus Christ and the gospel. To take the eternal gospel, wrap it in appropriate cultural garb, and make it accessible to people more efficiently than any other religion (or corporation) sounds to me like the challenge of a lifetime. Any takers?

Victor's reality check

In this parable, Victor, pastor of a rural church in Colombia, lands at O'Hare airport in Chicago and his host and hostess quickly show him how wonderful it is to be a Christian in America. They start with Christian radio and television and move on to their Christian books on every conceivable subject, plus Bible translations galore, Bible study helps, and curriculum materials. Next, their shelves of Christian audio and video cassettes.

They take him to their church and he is stunned by the bulletin. In addition to children's and youth groups, he finds special interest groups for new mothers, mothers-to-be, and single mothers, plus senior citizens, alcoholics, the abused, and the unemployed. He learns that the church pays people to lead the music and plan programs for children, junior and senior high kids, college students, singles, career people, and retired people. Of course, the building itself is thickly carpeted and air conditioned to the point of freezing him.

The congregation, he notices, is bombarded with appeals to go to seminars, workshops, camps, and conferences on a host of pragmatic subjects. He is dumbfounded by the opportunities for men, women, and children, and youth to go off on retreats. Envy assails him when he learns how many training opportunities pastors have.

Back at the house, he picks up a Christian magazine and sees ads for the Ultrathin Reference Bible, the New King James Version, which has spun off 13 major study Bibles from one publisher alone, the New Interpreter's Bible, the International Inductive Study Bible, the New

Revised Standard Bible, The Living Bible, the Ryrie Study Bible, the Weston Study Bible, plus ads for 13 different computer software programs designed to help people know their Bibles better.

What an orgy of good things to help Christians be everything Jesus and the apostles had in mind. This must be paradise, he thinks, or at least it's as close to heaven as you can get and still be here. Not only are these spiritual muscle builders on the market, but Christians actually buy them and go to the seminars.

Then Victor wonders about something he read about the distribution of global income. The richest 20 percent of the people in the world get 85 percent of the world's gross national product, while the poorest 20 percent get only 1 percent. Do American Christians get 85 percent or more of the world's Christian products? Perhaps so, based on what he's seen.

But, at the church's missions conference, he hears that new missionaries lack support to go and returned missionaries have fallen behind in support. The church just can't afford to add even one dollar to its missions budget, what with the building fund debt, increased staff salaries, and so many people out of work.

Where is reality? he wonders. Victor listens patiently as someone explains that the world is pretty much evangelized, missionaries aren't needed or welcomed any more, "native" missionaries can do it cheaper, and, above all, we've got lots of needs here at home.

Victor asks himself, If these Christians actually are using their profusion of resources for growth, and if they are studying their study Bibles, why aren't they turning the world upside down in their own communities? Why aren't they acting like the church at Antioch? Why can't they see that they have so much and we in Colombia have so little? Can't they see the gross imbalance, or unfairness, in the allocation of Christian resources? Why should American Christians have so much and Colombian Christians so little? Why can't they see that people in the U.S. have so many more chances to hear about Jesus, compared to our people?

What shall we tell him?

What can sink world missions

Some 1,500 Haitians crammed into the old, rusty, overloaded ferry *Neptune* for the 11-hour trip from Jérémie to Port-au-Prince. Twelve hundred of them drowned on February 17, 1993. They could have taken the bus, except that Haiti's roads have virtually disappeared because of neglect, and the cost of fuel has skyrocketed due to an international embargo imposed after the military coup in 1991.

To put the problem in modern jargon, Haiti's infrastructure has largely collapsed. Not that it was ever very sturdy. For nearly 200 years the despots who have governed Haiti have not given the proverbial two hoots about roads, water, sewers, schools, or electricity. Said one anthropologist, "The notion of government-provided services has never reached the majority of the Haitian population, and it is certainly not the sense that the Haitian ruling classes have of the role of government."

Twelve hundred people perished mostly because the people who could have made a difference didn't. They didn't care about degenerate roads, lack of affordable fuel, and ferries running way beyond capacity, without either lifeboats or life jackets. "To anybody who cared, it was a disaster just waiting to happen," said a U.S. Coast Guard official. Ah, there's the rub. Who cares?

Starvation in Somalia? Wicked persecution in Sudan? Brutalization of Bosnians? Bombings and kidnappings in Peru and Colombia? Indiscriminate shelling in Kabul? Who cares? It's not my problem.

Some 950,000 Komering of Indonesia have never heard of Jesus? Eight hundred thousand Qashqa'i in southern Iran unevangelized? Who cares? It's not my problem.

Unfortunately, what sank the *Neptune* and took 1,200 Haitians to eternity can also sink world missions. If we don't keep our missionary "roads" in good repair, we won't be able to get missionaries from here to there and back. If we don't provide reasonable "fuel," potential missionaries will rot on the vine like tomatoes after a September frost. If we don't provide lifeboats and life jackets, when disaster strikes many missionaries will go down. Worst of all, if we keep saying, "Who cares? It's not my problem," we'll sink like the *Neptune*, overloaded by all of our stuff that keeps us from sensing God's heartbeat for a world of perishing people.

Could it be that the vessel christened by Jesus, which we call world missions, has some Jonahs on board? How many Christians are running away from a blistering, swelling, pain-racked world? "Not my problem," they say. "Let the missionaries take care of it."

Of course, not every Christian is called to preach repentance in Nineveh, like Jonah was. But every Christian can be a pick and shovel worker on the roads, so that other fellow Christians can travel to distant, unevangelized people with a minimum of delay. This means, among other things, giving the money needed for home office managers, recruiters, trainers, secretaries, and receipt processors. Every Christian can be sure every missionary has enough fuel to burn. This means giving adequate support to cover extremely high costs of living overseas. Every Christian can be an emotional and spiritual lifeboat for missionaries dangerously close to being swept overboard by discouragement, illness, and satanic opposition. This means praying with muscle and sweat.

The missionary road from here to there will always be mined by the enemy, or saturated with potholes, or riddled with ruts. Remember how the Viet Cong frustrated the U.S. bombing of the Ho Chi Minh trail from North to South Vietnam? They did it by pouring thousands of pick and shovel people into the bomb craters every day, endangering their lives for the sake of keeping that vital road open. No one dared say, "It's not my problem."

Our confused world, seemingly unable to extricate itself from horrendous tragedies, is our problem. We must care deeply about keeping the road "from Jerusalem to Irian Jaya" open at all costs.

When the house is on fire

Our nightly television fare is as predictable as a McDonald's menu. While we wait vainly for significant reports about what's happening overseas, we're fed a steady diet of fires, crashes, and murders. Not only is the news predictable, so is its coverage. The most gripping shots show relatives weeping over young murder victims, and distraught mothers screaming at firemen to save their children from a house engulfed in flames. Your emotions wrung out, you stare blankly at the screen, totally stripped of any feeling for the suffering. Are the legions who have enlisted for world missions similarly desensitized?

One day in Jerusalem Peter stood before thousands of people and told them their house was on fire, so to speak, and they had better flee for their lives. I am concerned that so much of what we do under the missions umbrella seems to lack both Peter's focus and passion. We risk stripping "mission" and "missionary" of his pentecostal zeal and fervor.

How dissimilar our attitude is compared to Peter's, the freshly minted evangelist. Here was the coward who denied Jesus boldly declaring to Jews and proselytes from all over the world that "God has made this Jesus, whom you crucified, both Lord and Messiah."

How can we recapture his spirit and put proclamation at the heart of everything we do? How can we force all missionaries and their managers to scrutinize all their activities and expenditures under the searchlight of provocative, loving, forthright gospeling?

By following Peter's spiritual trail. He saw and listened to Jesus after his resurrection. Next, he was overwhelmed by the Holy Spirit. Finally, as he gazed on thousands of people gathered in Jerusalem for Pentecost, he saw them neither as enemies nor cold statistics but as human beings living in mortal danger. That's when his emotions took over.

Peter acted like the mother standing on the street knowing her children are dying in flames. As I read

Peter's sermon I imagine him surely shouting, with tears in his eyes, "Save yourselves!" We have a distillation of Peter's sermon, but the heart and soul of what he did was tersely captured by Luke: Peter pressed his case and pleaded with the crowd with many words, like the terrified mother pleading with the firefighters to save her children.

Going on a mission means being sent by God to press and plead with people to repent and confess Jesus Christ as Lord and Savior. Somehow Peter's urgency and passion must spill out of our offices, field conferences, and consultations like a raging flood smashing everything in its way. Peter's passion must funnel everything we do toward courageously proclaiming the name of Jesus to the ends of the earth.

Why don't we press and plead our case like Peter? Because in what we call our mission work we do so many other important and good things. However, they dilute what "mission" and "missionary" are supposed to mean. We will continue like this as long as we are impervious to the precipice of devastating loss that looms ahead. We will not send people to cry, "Save yourselves!" unless we believe there is a terrible destiny from which all people need to be saved. Their houses really are on fire.

Such single-minded passion does not spring from a TV set. Only when we see people as Peter did will we attempt courageous, risky, bold things in all corners of the earth. Then we will press the case for Christ's lordship and plead with people to repent and believe.

Why fish?

The fisherman was in a tight spot trying to explain to a lady why he fished. She was incensed by the brutality of fishing. He felt like a fish impaled on a treble barbed hook. He squirmed and tried to shake her off, but to no avail. He didn't think the few fish he caught and kept had been brutalized. He released most of his catches. But she kept badgering him for reasons why he fished at all.

Seeing that he was not going to persuade his antagonist, he surrendered. He realized that nothing he could say would have changed her mind. Later on, under less hostile circumstances he began to think of a host of good reasons why he like to fish. Killing fish was not on his list.

I wondered how Peter, James, and John—fishermen all—would have answered people who asked them why they were fishing for people instead of fish. They had left their fishing business because Jesus called them to join him in fishing for people. "Come with me, and I will teach you to catch men," he said.

Whenever we think about what the church should be doing in the world, we have to answer the question, Why fish? What would the disciples have answered? Probably without any hesitation they would have said, "Because Jesus told us to."

They lived day to day, hand to mouth, trying to catch people because Jesus said he would teach them to do it. He not only gave them lessons, he showed them how to do it. He sent them out two by two to fish. What magnificent fishing lessons we find in the four Gospels.

They fished in a small pond at first, but later on Jesus

told them their pond was the entire world. Christians fish for people in every country and culture, among people of all languages and ethnic distinctives, among people of every religion and no religion. They fish in places posted with NO FISHING signs, because Jesus did not limit his directives according to political and religious barriers. So we have some very creative fishing going on in some hazardous ponds.

Perhaps if we had traveled for some time with Jesus and his fishermen, they would have added, "We're fishing because people need to be caught." Think about the multiplicity of needs they encountered—the sick and demon-possessed, the exploited and rejected, lepers and prostitutes, grief-stricken people who had lost children, crippled and chronically ill people, blind people, and tax collectors who had cheated people. The disciples knew that if they fished for these people and brought them to Jesus they would be caught. Not by trickery or manipulation, but by love and forgiveness.

Later on, perhaps, they could have said they were fishing because God's kingdom was about to break in upon them. Something startlingly new was about to happen. Old, rigid patterns and beliefs would be shattered. They realized that they were fishing for God's Son, the promised Messiah, and that his glory would be revealed as they fished. They were in step with God's eternal redemptive plan for the world.

Every Christian and every church ought to be able to answer the question, Why fish? If we cannot answer it simply and clearly, we are missing what Jesus calls us to do. His call is not limited to professional fishermen. He wants the shores and banks of every river and lake to be lined with his people learning how to catch people.

We fish because Jesus told us to fish, because people need him, and because God's kingdom and glory demand that we do. The world is our pond.

The Call

Lesson from a favorite: "Don't quit"

One of my all-time favorite missionaries, **William McElwee Miller, has gone to glory.** He would have been 101 years old in December, 1993. A real Hall of Famer, he has received his richly deserved crown of glory. He ran the race with patience and pressed on to win the prize, not on Easy Street, but in Iran among people whom 30 years ago we were told to give up on because they were "resistant."

Rising to contain that stream of thinking, in 1976 he wrote his classic, *A Christian's Response to Islam*. In his final chapter, Miller cogently and boldly declared 16 reasons for continuing missions to Muslims. At age 97, he wrote his lesser known but intensely personal story, *My Persian Pilgrimage*.

I first met William Miller in the 1960s, when he had retired to Philadelphia after 43 years of service as a Presbyterian missionary in Iran. I felt I was in the presence not only of a man who walked with God, but whose graciousness truly gave off the aroma of Christ. He was a true gentleman of the old school. As I later learned in several conversations with him, he was also a fascinating link with great missionary statesmen of the past, such as Robert E. Speer, whom I had only read about.

If there ever was a Heartbreak Hill in missions, it's Muslim evangelism and church planting. William Miller shunned bragging, but he always hoped that his stories about Muslim converts would encourage young people not only to work among Muslims, but to stay at it.

People often ask why reaching Muslims is as hard as

removing a nut from a rusty bolt. There are many reasons, none of which ever quenched William Miller's enthusiasm as he criss-crossed Iran with the gospel. In those days (1919-62) he enjoyed the relative luxury of unhindered literature distribution and evangelism, but he and his family paid a heavy price for every Muslim who came to faith in Christ.

When he wrote about it, he did not exalt sacrifice and hardship, preferring rather, as the apostle Paul did, to see these things as privileges and blessings. "I would say that anything that has been done, was not done by me, but by Christ who called me to his service, and in mercy has enabled me, during a long life, to bear some fruit for him," he wrote.

We are losers in missions today if we choose to ignore or, in some cases, even resent the stories of those who have served with distinction. In some circles, we hear complaints about missionary heroes, because, we are told, the world has changed and people are different today. We can't go back to horse-and-buggy missions, they say.

Of course, the world has changed, and missionary work has changed with it, but some abiding principles of faithfulness and unwavering commitment to hard tasks do not change, whether in missions or anything else. Between the discovery of the cause of tuberculosis and the discovery of a cure, for example, more than 70 years passed. The experts didn't believe it would ever be cured, so the amateurs persisted, and half of them weren't even medically qualified.

The idea of staying at something for a long time is truly countercultural. Even as I write this, I feel as if I'm out of sync with the world, which tells us to move on if things don't work out. That kind of thinking, along with a quick-fix pragmatism, has seriously infected world missions.

If William Miller could say one thing to today's missionaries, it probably would be, "Don't quit." He would also say the same thing to those who pray for and support them.

Making life our priority

Every Monday night the guys who lived in the University Christian Union at the University of Washington in Seattle were summoned by our house parent, Charles (Chief) Peterson, to discuss our efforts in personal evangelism.** Like a farmer collecting eggs, he expected us to produce. Chief always asked, "Any stories?" The peer pressure worked.

The UCU house was not a Christian ghetto, but a base from which we were to evangelize the university. Chief Peterson himself set the pace. (This was long before books about mentoring were written.) After we told our stories, Chief told his own, fresh from the front lines downtown where he worked.

In one, he had initiated a daily conversation with his regular parking lot attendant. It was short, simple, but enigmatic: "Have you got life?" The man was puzzled and usually talked about religion. Chief never argued or persuaded. He just tried to show the man that the issue was not religion, but life in Jesus Christ.

One morning, after a month of this, as Chief pulled into the lot the man dashed up to him, yelling, "I've got life! I've got life!" To me, this is much more than a story about how to witness to our faith. Sure, we were all thrilled and rejoiced when Chief told us the outcome. But we learned that the essence of mission and evangelism is life.

Jesus said, "I am the way and the truth and the life . . . . I am the resurrection and the life. . . . I have come that they might have life, and have it to the full."

Yes, life is the main thing. It is what we are about, bringing life to people dead in their trespasses and sins. The gift of God is eternal life. Life is found in Jesus Christ and in no one else. If this sounds like the Old Fashioned Revival Hour, so be it. We need to know and act like the only thing on our mission agenda is life. A truly biblical mission agenda is not littered with a laundry list of good things Christians do. It's not strangled by a host of things charitable organizations do, worthy as they may be. Once we have choked life with machinery to run programs, we have missed what we are supposed to do.

Having spent hundreds of hours on mission agendas, I can tell you where much of our time, energy, and thought go. Not into producing life among the dead, but into mission business: personnel and support, property and taxes, relations with our partners overseas, and fund raising and recruiting at home. When will we wake up? The question is not, Where are we going to get money, recruits, buildings, and property? but, How many people are finding life in Jesus Christ? Does everybody in this mission organization know, believe, and act like life is the only issue?

What would we say at our international councils, field councils, and U.S. councils if we were asked for stories? What stories do our church-planting teams have? Our secretaries, pilots, radio technicians, nurses, teachers, linguists, accountants, well drillers, and relief workers? If we do not tell stories about people finding life in Christ, we ought to reconsider our purposes.

I once sailed across a fog-bound bay off the coast of Maine. We could see nothing, but the consistent clanging of the bells on the channel markers split the fog and kept us on course. The New Testament's channel marker is eternal life in Christ. That bell must crash around our ears and pierce the fog of irrelevance, or we will drift off into a sea of good-intentioned but meaningless mission business.

Plague-spreading Christians

Remember some of those old cliches we used to hear at missionary conferences: "You're either a mission field or a missionary!" "If you aren't called to stay, you're called to go!" I've often wondered how many people heard God's call despite the faulty theology of those well-meaning slogans. Anyway, I've come up with a new one that I think has some biblical validity: "Every Christian should be a plague-spreading Christian!"

Now that the plague has revisited the planet, we have a perfect model of how the gospel originally infected the world, and how it should continue to do so. The plague suddenly struck Surat, India, and despite frantic efforts it soon spread to other parts of the country. Now health officials at airports around the world are checking arrivals for the plague. Wouldn't it be something if Christians of all nations were so infectious with the gospel?

My point is that it's bunk to suggest Christians ought

to go to the mission field if they're not called to stay home, or that anyone who is a Christian (i.e., not a mission field) is automatically a missionary. But it is gospel truth that all those who have been infected by the Jesus plague ought to pass it on to others. That doesn't make them missionaries, just obedient disciples of Jesus.

Somewhere along the line our thinking got badly fuzzed by the notion that anything we do for Jesus qualifies as "missionary" work. Your neighbor breaks his leg and you take him to the clinic. Does that make you a missionary? Of course not. It makes you a kind person, not a missionary.

Furthermore, our thinking also got scrambled by the heresy that only missionaries, pastors, and evangelists are carriers of the Jesus plague. That was a winner, because it conveniently excused hordes of Christians from their responsibility to spread the Jesus plague, too. God does not call every believer to be a missionary, but he does call all of Christ's disciples to spread the Jesus plague.

One of the reasons Christians find it uncomfortable even to ask God if they should be missionaries is that they've never been good at spreading the Jesus plague. They like to cheer the plague spreaders to foreign shores, but please don't ask them to spread it to the folks next door. They get excited about an outbreak of the Jesus plague in Mauritania, but get mad when the Muslims take over their local Dunkin' Donuts shop.

Hard as we may try, we cannot sever the lifeline between local and foreign plague carriers. You cannot send plague carriers overseas unless the church is full of plague carriers here. Eventually the Jesus plague will die out, unless all Christians spread it next door and everywhere. Nobody will want to carry it overseas because nobody cares enough to carry it next door. Oh, the overseas carriers will go on for a little while longer, but when they expire no one will take their places, because the churches—even the so-called "missions-minded" churches—didn't spread the Jesus plague in their own backyards.

In the Philippines, where hundreds of thousands hire out for work in other countries, the churches train the Christians among them how to be Jesus plague carriers wherever they go. There are more house servants among them than businessmen and scientists, but they are very good at spreading the Jesus plague.

On any given day scores of American Christians arrive in virtually every airport in the world. They are not missionaries, but they should carry the Jesus plague. Wouldn't it be something if they somehow radiated Jesus so brilliantly that they set off alarms at the baggage X-ray checkpoints? Before they go, we have to identify them as plague carriers and tell them how to infect others. They, too, are part of God's commitment and strategy to save the world.

Prayerless in Colombia

First, our government said to the Colombians, "Sorry, boys, we're not going to give you any more money, because you haven't licked the drug cartel." Next, the Colombians screamed and hollered about how unjust this was, and then shot dead their No. 3 drug honcho. Our relations with Colombia in 1996 are as sour as early green apples.

But while U.S. foreign aid and Colombia's drug barons grabbed the headlines for a few days, four U.S. missionary captives continued to languish in Colombia's jungles. Unfortunately, this latest diplomatic dust-up will further muddy efforts to secure the release of hostages Ray Rising, Dave Mankins, Mark Rich, and Rick Tenenoff.* Instead, it probably increases the risk of violence. Whatever leverage the U.S. government had with the Colombians to deal with the guerrillas for the release of the four men has crashed like the American Airlines 757 going into Cali.

Yet nobody pays attention, neither the diplomats nor the Christians in North America. I would have thought that one of the networks would have picked up this story by now. In fact, the families of the hostages have urged them to do so. But so far nothing has appeared on the evening news. Broadcasters rightly say it's extremely dangerous to send TV cameramen into Colombia, but danger didn't stop them in Vietnam and Iraq.

It's disgraceful that our churches and Christian media have not joined forces to mobilize public prayer and support for these men and their families. Three of them have been held by Colombian guerrillas for more than three years; the fourth for more than two years.

What stops us from doing or saying anything is a tragic lack of concern for the victims, their wives, children, siblings, and parents. We see pictures almost every day of dozens of people being blown up somewhere. Our culture is over-victimized, so what's the big deal about four men we really don't know? To most people, their reasons for being in Colombia don't make much sense anyway.

Pressure is on the State Department and the Colombian government is a lost cause, but what about pressure on our churches to pray? Lost cause? Seems to be. These four men are virtual unknowns in our pulpits. Never hear anything about them on the Christian TV and radio shows that command audiences of millions.

The only ripple comes from the mission agencies behind the men. However, we need more than ripples, we need a tidal wave. But the longer their cases drag on, the less concern we have for persistent daily prayer for them. We need consistent prayer in our pulpits and from our Christian media superstars.

I confess it's hard to engage in daily intercession for people you don't know. But that didn't stop us from praying when people we didn't know were being held hostage in Iran and Lebanon. Last year I was preaching and praying regularly in the same church on Sunday mornings. After several months of praying publicly for the hostages by name, one person caught on and said to me, "You really care about those people, don't you?"

That's what it all boils down to, doesn't it? If we care, we'll pray; if we don't, we won't. If God's view of world missions means anything at all, it means caring and praying—not indifference, callousness, and prayerlessness.

*Rising was eventually released. The other three are still missing.

Prayer's preeminence

Prayer requests flood my e-mail circuits. Rather than print them out and forget them, I pray while I read them on the screen. That's one way I pray for missionaries. I also organize my regular missionary praying around continents. Some people keep prayer notebooks. Missionary prayer circles compile letters and e-mails. However we do it, prayer is work.

I marvel at how often the apostle Paul asked his friends to pray for him. He encouraged them never to stop praying. His own prayers unmask the shallowness of ours. God desires prayer because he longs for our fellowship. Prayer lies at the heart of his plan for world missions and evangelism. But until we pray, our knowledge of these facts condemns us as hypocrites. God hates hypocrisy. We may boast about how many missionaries we send and the size of our missionary budgets, but those numbers ring hollow if we do not obey God's will and pray. God spoke to Isaiah about the veneer of prosperous but phony religion. Underneath, things smelled so bad that God said he hated Israel's prayers, offerings, and sacrifices.

Prayer's preeminence and practice stand out in many churches and on many campuses. Stories coming out of college prayer groups describe hours of intercession for people who have no churches and no witness. I have sat in Wednesday night prayer circles, and in men's prayer meetings, where prayers ascend for missionaries by name.

Friends recently told me about a spontaneous prayer group started by people in their church. This group gathers in homes and they pray until one and two o'clock in the morning. But in many churches prayer has all but disappeared. Our technological age looks for answers elsewhere. Churches can easily be diverted from prayer by important, useful programs.

Missions committees look for better mousetraps to revitalize missionary vision and interest. How hard it is to remember the basics and start with prayer.

Theologically, we're convinced that God has the answers. He has ideas we've never dreamed about. But often we prefer action to prayer. We're like Saul, who could not wait for the prophet Samuel, and lost his kingdom.

Prayer is grueling, demanding, sacrificial work. Prayer causes us to rearrange our priorities. Prayer causes us to think about God and his purposes. Prayer relieves and disturbs us. Prayer is the vital food for our souls. Prayer requires up-to-date facts. That's why e-mail is such a boon to missionary prayer.

I've never been much good at telling people how to pray. Prayer seems to bubble forth from some unseen spring when people love God more than anything else. I know I must keep telling myself that I fail God, my missionary friends, and myself when I do not pray.

Prayer is partnership with God and with those he has sent into world missions. He calls some to do the hard work in the harvest fields. He calls all of us to do the hard work of prayer.

Whatever it takes, we must make time to pray. I learned early on that I could not compete with the prayer warriors who spend hours at a time on their knees. But I found that I could meet with God satisfactorily in shorter bursts. One of the most memorable days I have ever spent was a Saturday of fasting and prayer called by our church at the request of one of our missionaries. Many people learned for the first time that they could do it, not by praying all day but by committing themselves to pray during specific blocks of time. Many believers and churches do this regularly.

However we do it, prayer must come first. If prayer is not preeminent, nothing else really counts.

Protection from what?

The missionary's letter concluded with fairly typical prayer requests: Pray for the new seekers. Pray for safety and protection. Certainly valid, considering the country he and his wife work in. Prayer is absolutely essential for this family, because prayer partnership between home and field is as critical as communication between flight controllers and airline pilots.

But I wonder if their requests and our prayers for them miss the mark. Protection from what? From robbers and burglars, crazy drivers, and diseases. In many places, protection from terrorists and kidnappers.

If we really pressed our missionary friends, they would come up with a different list. They face some dangers that are much more important than those they write home about. For starters, they need protection from Satan's attacks on their faith and calling. Sometimes they are tempted to quit and go home. They need God to protect their marriages and families. They need protection from doing so much work that they neglect their families.

They need God's protection of their most priceless privilege, their time. "Lord, protect them from getting so busy doing things for you, that they forget to take time to sit and listen to you. They forget to find unhurried time for Bible meditation and prayer. Protect them from losing their spirit of worship, love, and devotion for you."

Missionaries greatly need protection from divisiveness, criticism, and crankiness with each other. "Lord, protect their unity in Christ. Protect their love for each other. Protect their commitment to each other. Protect their willingness to serve one another, and to esteem their sisters and brothers better than themselves."

They certainly need protection from conflicts with local believers and national church leaders. Protection from squabbling over budgets and properties. Protection from misinterpreting each other's motives. Protection from even hinting that the way we do it in America is best. Protection from using their control of money to get their own way.

Jesus did ask God to protect his disciples, but not the kind of protection we usually think of. He had warned them they would be dragged out of synagogues and killed, so he did not pray for their safety and protection from persecution, or, as we might say, terrorists. Jesus simply asked his Father to protect the disciples "so that they be one as we are one." They needed protection from infighting, jealousy, and clamoring for position. Unity in Christ, with each other, and with local national believers, ranked higher in Jesus' prayer than safety.

Unity among missionaries is so important because as unbelievers watch them, they will see and grasp the good news that God loves them so much that he sent Jesus to this world.

Jesus also prayed that God would protect his disciples from the evil one. He said he had protected them, and all of them were safe except Judas. Safe from what? Defection. Their greatest need was the protection of their souls, not their bodies. Saving faith outranks physical safety. Our primary prayer concern for our missionaries should be their perseverance in faith.

If the evil one cannot destroy their faith, he will disrupt their work by sowing dissension in their ranks. If he can get our missionaries to believe gossip and suspect each other's motives, Satan does not have to resort to terrorism. If he can maneuver them into head-on collisions with the national believers, he doesn't need car crashes to wipe them out.

Our missionaries ask, "Pray for our safety and protection." Of course. But, we have to pray like Jesus did, and keep first things first.

Rejoice! Are you kidding?

God's timing begs explanation and understanding. Relaxed as a blossoming cloud welcoming the dawn, I mulled over "Rejoice in the Lord always. I will say it again: Rejoice!" It was, in fact, early morning when I read the apostle's puzzling protocol. Always? Surely that isn't possible, is it? But circumstances at day's beginning made it relatively simple to agree with Paul.

Radically, rudely, roughly the circumstances changed within an hour or so. The pink "While You Were Out" message sheet on my desk hammered me like a blast from a Winchester 30.06. Norm and Ginny gone? Just like that? I swallowed hard and had to admit the terrible truth. Rejoice always? Surely you jest, Paul.

Our best efforts to evangelize the world often seem to crash like that Romanian jet. Six missionaries languish as hostages in Colombia. Dollar-dependent missionaries in Japan tighten their belts another notch. Missionary refugees from Rwanda can't make the pieces fit.

Of course, the man who told us to rejoice in the Lord always was not a stranger to hardships that seemingly made it impossible to rejoice. Stoned, shipwrecked, and jailed, Paul nevertheless plumbed a reservoir of confidence somewhere in his being that enabled him to stay on track.

Perhaps we stumble over this paradox because we suffer from misguided notions about rejoicing. Certainly Paul did not mean that we should jump up and down with gleeful abandon, like a bunch of kids at a peanut scramble, when our friends go down in a plane crash. In fact, according to the New Testament, joy is not a supermarket commodity.

—Consider it pure joy whenever you face trials?

—Rejoice in our sufferings?

—Jesus for the joy set before him endured the cross?

—Rejoice, though now for a little while you may suffer grief in all kinds of trials?

When we trace the records of God's mysterious ways in world evangelism, it's not unusual to find the church crawling ahead like a battered infantryman into enemy territory. The church rarely, if ever, advances behind flags waving and bugles blaring.

Could it be, then, that as the church and her missionaries rejoice in the midst of unfathomable obstacles and calamities, people catch a glimpse of spiritual power that supersedes words alone? Jesus said he would draw people to him when they saw him lifted up on a cross.

The paradox of rejoicing in the cross—whatever that may mean for us—could very well be the explosive ingredient the church needs when we strategize about reaching people who've never heard or understood the gospel. Our councils of war many times seem to flaunt assumptions of power, not of plane crashes, massacres, and wildly fluctuating currencies. On the front lines, in mission board rooms, and in church missions committees, it's easy to rejoice when good reports come flooding in like truckloads of grain to the loading dock. But what do we do when the harvest is sparse, or nonexistent? What signals do we send then?

Will we find God himself to be our joy, like Habakkuk did? "Though the fig tree does not bud and there are not grapes on the vines, though the olive crop fails and the fields produce no food, though there are no sheep in the pen and no cattle in the stalls, yet will I rejoice in the Lord, I will be joyful in God my Savior." How contrary to much spurious, sub-Christian thinking today.

Yes, rejoice, and don't worry, but pray instead. God's peace—which we can't understand anyway—will rise up and throw a magnificent wall around us. God did that for me; not the first time, of course, and not the last.

So you want to be a missionary?*

Be sure you are sent by the owner of the harvest— the Lord Jesus Christ—to work in his fields. You will go because his harvest is bountiful and his workers are scarce. You will go because others have prayed for you to be sent by him.

Be sure you have Jesus' authority to do his work. You must be in step with the Lord's program, policies, and practices. This is much more important than having some organization's authority to do its work.

Be sure Jesus knows you by name, and that he knows all about you, warts and all. You are his companion and friend. He wants to live in you and bear fruit in, within, and through you. You are his plan and program to bring in his harvest.

Be sure you know Jesus' commission and the message he wants you to proclaim. You will find this only in closest communion with him in his words and in prayer. Your calling is to listen before you work, to meditate before you lift a hand.

Be sure you know the full scope of working in the harvest, because the fields are full of helpless, harassed, hurting people for whom few others—especially those in power—have any compassion at all. Their needs are total—spiritual and physical. They must be touched as well as taught, brought to spiritual life in God's kingdom as well as to physical wholeness and health here and now.

Be sure you know that working for Jesus is not work for hire. You did not earn your way onto his work force, and therefore you must not expect wages from him.

Be sure you trust Jesus to give you all you need to survive in the fields. Don't load yourself up with a lot of stuff you think you will need.

Be sure you learn from Jesus how to size up the harvest. Pray to enter the lives of those who will welcome you. Don't be surprised, however, because some parts of the field are not ripe. In fact, some people will reject the workers who bring peace.

Be sure you know you will be working like a sheep among wolves. You will work in weakness, not power. Ask Jesus to teach you how to survive and be a proficient harvester, despite the risks of being caught off guard, or trusting your own cleverness.

Be sure you are prepared for persecution at the hands of religious and political leaders. This will be for the sake of Jesus, so you can testify to him. This is a tough way to harvest, but it is the Lord's way. The Holy Spirit will speak through you, so don't worry about this in advance.

Be sure you are prepared for frightful consequences of your harvesting. Not everyone will be happy. Families will be split by betrayals and even death. You will be hated for your allegiance to Jesus, but don't quit because he will save you. If persecution in one place gets really bad, go to another place.

Be sure you don't put yourself above Jesus. Expect to share his lot in every way. He didn't come for appreciation, respect, and power. He came to seek and to save the lost, and for that he was called the devil. He said his workers should expect much worse.

These are not my instructions. They come from Jesus himself (Matt. 9:35-10:25).

---

*(1) short-term missionary (usually a few weeks); (2) short-term specialized missionary (up to six months); (3) short-term support missionary (six months to two years); (4) contract missionary (pioneer work for five to 10 years); (5) tentmaker missionary (one to five years); (6) long-term missionary (career commitment).

The cross keeps us in the race

Stepping it off around the park one afternoon on my usual path, I was nearly flattened by a horde of guys clad in shorts, jerseys, and sneakers. They thundered around the bend like they meant business, so I quickly dodged out of their way. Once the front-runners disappeared, I got back on the track and met the panting stragglers in this high school cross-country race. They weren't nearly so dangerous. From across the way came the voices of screaming teammates, urging these desperately dragged out boys not to quit.

Cross-country racing is a strenuous test of fitness and endurance. It's probably closer to the original concept of athletic competition in the minds of the Greeks than football will ever be. Greek athletes competed fiercely for a simple laurel wreath, not for multimillion-dollar contracts. Footraces preceded the other four contests of the pentathlon. Olympic athletes had to swear by Zeus to follow 10 months of strict training.

Paul said he wanted to push himself to the limit to win the prize for which God had called him. He told Timothy that he had fought the good fight and finished his race, so he anticipated receiving his crown from Jesus. Not only is personal devotion a battle (Paul wanted to be sure he kept the faith), but so is our obedience to God's saving purposes among the nations.

The biblical epic moves from one person (Abraham) to the universal victory celebration that will bring together God's people from all languages, colors, races, and nationalities. God's people are inseparably linked with Jesus in a cosmic battle, the outcome of which has already been decided. Paul reminded his fledgling church at Colossae that on the cross Jesus did not lose, he won.

There is no athletic metaphor for something like this. So Paul took them back to the dreadful scene of mighty Roman legions bringing their chain-ganged captives into town for the victory celebration. On the cross Jesus took the worst that hell could throw at him and cast off the powers of darkness like so much dirty laundry. Beyond that, Christ made a public spectacle of these discarded cosmic powers and led them as captives in his triumphal parade.

The struggle raging for our minds, hearts, and wills is a microcosm of heaven's warfare for the destiny of all people and nations. On our way to Christ's celebration we engage worldwide powers in religion, politics, business, academics, and entertainment, for example. These powers think they are strong, but Paul reminds us that every power and authority in the universe is subject to Jesus.

Sometimes, it seems that we do a lot of cheerleading in world missions. It's as though world evangelization is like a game we get pumped up for with a lot of this-worldy gimmicks. We plead for more runners, for bigger, stronger athletes, for bigger budgets to run the whole operation, for more people to take more trips, and for flashier promotions.

However, great peril looms ahead if we go down this road. Enormous risks confront us if we lose sight of Jesus on his cross. His cross must be central in every aspect of missionary endeavor. His cross not only towers over the wrecks of time, as the hymn puts it, it also towers over the wrecks of Christian missions.

The cross compels us to enlist in the Jesus cause in the first place. The cross guarantees the outcome of the battle. Submitting everything we do to the searchlight of the cross will keep us in the race until we receive our crowns from the Lord Jesus Christ.

The pierced ear

Staring at the back of the head in the pew in front **of me, I wasn't sure if it was male or female.** The tiny gold earring stuck in the left ear lobe caught my eye first, but that was inconclusive. I had to be sure, so I searched the right ear lobe. No earring. Sure enough, it was a boy, about 14. (Yes, I tried to "make a statement," as they now say, when I was 14, but wearing an earring was not the way to do it then. So instead I wore my in-famous "monkey tie.")

I cannot precisely interpret what pierced ears and ear-rings say for boys (and men) today, but I do know what the pierced ear said in the days of Moses. It marked a devoted lifelong servant. Every missionary should be-long to "the order of the pierced ear," so to speak, be-cause today the notion of lifelong missionary service is getting plowed under by our prevailing cultural attitudes toward careers and vocations in general.

Phil is one of the old order, a veteran of 30 years in some of the world's toughest places, where gratification does not come from huge numbers of converts. He's got a pierced ear for Jesus and for the cause of making him known in hostile territory. Like John Wayne riding, crawling, and slugging it out to capture the villains of the Old West, Phil has stayed with his primary task.

Why? A paragraph from his last prayer letter says it all: "Often we are asked about our future plans. Attrac-tive offers to teach and administer in the States have come and gone. None have ever really enticed us. We are very, very happy (where we are). My life's motif is to 'persevere to the end with integrity.'"

That's the pierced ear motif. Why are pierced ears be-coming scarcer and scarcer in world missions? Some would say it's because today's newcomers belong to a generation that tries on jobs like someone posturing in Marshall Field's hat department. Others think it's be-cause nobody makes lifetime commitments to anything anymore, not even to marriage, let alone to some Chris-tian vocation like being a pastor or a missionary.

Another theory says it's unrealistic to expect this of missionaries in today's world because conditions on the field change so rapidly (civil wars, visa restrictions, and so on), and the national churches don't want you to stay around for life anyway. Being a lifelong missionary is a false hope, some say, because of changing family demands (taking care of elderly parents, educating your children, and so on), to say nothing of health and financial risks.

None of this is new. Missionaries have always had to change their field of service for these reasons, and some have always had to come home. But that was not their intention when they started out. What we are seeing more of today are the intentional short-term expectations of new missionaries, not the lifelong commitment denoted by the pierced ear.

Is this trend caused by a mysterious spiritual malaise descending upon our homes, churches, and schools, like deadly carbon monoxide escaping from your furnace? Perhaps so. Perhaps almost unconsciously we have succumbed to the noxious fumes that lure us to think that we can carry on world missions on a purely secular basis.

Do we give the impression that being a missionary is just like any other career, or vocation, and if it doesn't work out, you can move into something else? In our zeal to attract recruits, do we lower the demands just a little, lest we risk turning some away? Jesus never did that, nor should we.

Far better to have a few devoted lifelong servants with their pierced ears, than a lot of people trying it out for a career fit. To that end, we need some resounding teaching, preaching, writing, and encouraging among the youth of America. We must refuse to allow culture to set the agenda for tomorrow's would-be missionaries.

Nothing less than having your ear nailed to the wall will do.

The towel and the basin

When I was a youngster my mother took me to an Old Order River Brethren love feast in a barn in **Lancaster County, Pa.** I sat quietly on a bench and listened to the hymns and sermons. My grandfather confessed his sins and was restored to fellowship. Then the members washed each other's feet. My uncle was a member. Finally, we were excused to the tables laden with simple food.

Whenever I read John 13, I recall that incident and regret the arguments about whether Jesus intended foot washing to be an abiding ordinance in the church. I don't have strong feelings either way, because the issue I have to deal with is my pride, not my church's traditions. I have to confess that had I been there in the Upper Room with Jesus, I would not have taken the basin and the towel. I would not have jumped at the chance to clean my fellow team members' dirty feet.

The word that stings is this: "If I, your teacher and Lord, have washed your feet, you must be ready to wash one another's feet." How could Jesus do this? Why did he do it? He did it because he was in control, even as his crucifixion loomed. He knew that he had come from God and that he was going to God. Knowing who he was, he took the servant's role. Self-identity powered humility.

He did it because he knew the success of his mission depended on his disciples' learning humility, love, and respect. He knew that unless they were willing to stoop to wash each other's feet, the church would die aborning.

Of course, in terms of contemporary church and mission life, we can say, "What a model of servant leadership!" Which is true, but I'm not sure Jesus had some theory of organizational management in mind. He was primarily interested in radically changing how his disciples saw themselves in his scheme of things. He promised them success on two counts: First, they had to grasp intellectually the enormity of what he had just done (God incarnate taking the towel and basin). "If I, the Son of God, have done this . . ." Second, they had to practice what he had done. Perhaps not in a ceremonial, ritualized way, but day in and day out as they rubbed shoulders in working out their post-Pentecost mission.

What this says to me in world missions is that everyone who tells the good news of the cross and resurrection must also be keenly aware of foot-washing opportunities. Perhaps some people we try to convert to Jesus would be more likely to listen to what we say if they saw us taking the basin and towel. This might even begin in language school with our fellow learners. It might begin in those precious early days of bonding with people whose lives we have entered as messengers from afar. Looking for chances to wash one another's feet would certainly do much to dispel our deeply ingrained notions of spiritual and technical superiority.

When we gather in our innumerable committees and conferences, how do we wash one another's feet? Are humility and service our chief concerns? Or are we out to make points and impress people? When we have washed one another's feet, somehow the rough edges disappear and the important stuff melts away into insignificance. In some cases, we may have to confess before we wash.

Perhaps we have been looking in the wrong places for answers to our problems. Perhaps the breakthroughs we pray for will come when we go back to the Upper Room with Jesus. There we can confess our insufferable pride and self-sufficiency, our own clever plans and strategies for success in our work—plans and strategies that somehow dodge the towel and the basin.

They knew where he had been

Pvt. Phendeus H. Potter, 9th New Hampshire Vol-unteers, took a slug through his jaw and mouth at Fredericksburg. Discharged because of his wounds, he walked back home from Maryland and became a preacher, a remarkable career choice, considering that his war injury had left him with severely impaired speech. But the people kept coming to hear him every Sunday, year after year, trying to grasp his words, because they knew where he had been.

Missionary work is nothing if it's not communication. Speaking the gospel so that it connects with hearers is as essential as laying the wood to a 90-mile-an-hour fastball, and just as difficult. To help them connect, missionaries study linguistics and culture. They spend time with people. They try to absorb their ways. They try to find common ground, some connectors to the real needs of the heart.

All the while, because they are aliens, they know they are as handicapped as Pvt. Potter was. Their American-isms are just as devastating as a bullet in the jaw. They can never get their own cultural baggage out of their systems. Not only is their message foreign, they themselves are and always will be foreigners.

To compensate, prospective missionaries are told to study more diligently, to take advanced degrees in missiology, anthropology, and linguistics. They read articles and books. They go to seminars, trying to find the latest techniques that will bring people to faith in Christ and establish them in churches. They are not told directly, but the implication is that if they master all their courses, books, and seminars they will be effective communicators.

At the risk of being called a pietistic obscurantist, I'd like to suggest that perhaps we are missing an essential component. Why did the people keep going to hear Preacher Potter, handicap and all? Because they knew where he had been. He had been in the frontlines; he had faced the enemy; he had wounds to prove it. There was nothing bookish about his knowledge of the war.

When missionaries land as aliens on a foreign shore, their would-be converts inspect them as carefully as El Al airlines security agents vacuum passengers' bodies and bags. But listeners aren't interested first in what degrees the missionaries have, or what they know about contextualization. They do look for some battlefield credentials. Classroom battles are fine, but missionaries need to take much more than their notes into the war for the souls of women and men. They have to take their scars.

What right have we to take the gospel elsewhere, if we haven't first carried the flag for Jesus right into the battles here at home? How many slugs have we taken, to harden us for really tough warfare in hostile territory?

Of course, missionaries need academic preparation, just like raw Army recruits need basic training. But effective missionary communicators must also have some battle ribbons pinned to their chests—before they get their 747 boarding passes. These ribbons can be earned evangelizing in the university world, among immigrants, in the cities among the poor and the well-to-do, in bypassed rural villages, and among our own neighbors in small Bible study groups as well as in prisons and hospitals, and among addicts, AIDS sufferers, the homeless, dropouts, and castoffs.

What have we done to earn the right to be heard? Why should anyone listen to us and our gospel? Why would anyone in unevangelized territory want to listen to an untested young American suburbanite?

Missionaries, despite their handicaps, must offer compelling signs of spiritual integrity and wholesomeness. At the trial of Peter and John before the Sanhedrin, two things were acknowledged about them by their accusers: their courage and their walk with Jesus. More than anything else, our listeners must receive unmistakable evidence that we have been with Jesus.

Two bullets and six gallons of gasoline

One by one our World War II heroes are passing away. Their obituaries ring down the memories like the clanging bells, flashing red lights, and lowering gates at railroad crossings, forcing us to stop, look, and listen.

David McCampbell was one of them. Aptly named

naval aviation's "Ace of Aces," McCampbell received the Medal of Honor for his exploits in the Pacific skies, where he shot down 34 Japanese planes.

In one battle he dispatched nine planes in 95 minutes, a tally believed to be the war's single-mission record. Afterwards, he landed with only two rounds of ammunition in his six machine guns and six gallons of gasoline in his tank—enough to keep his fighter in the air for 10 minutes.

Two bullets and six gallons of gasoline—and McCampbell wasn't worried. He was prepared for a long fight, but he had used his resources sparingly, and he knew he had enough to get home.

Do we have the same attitude toward our resources in world missions? Are we using them with superior knowledge and experience? Are we willing to go down to the last two bullets and six gallons of gasoline? Or do we build in comfortable safety margins?

There's a lot of talk today about corporations being lean and mean for the sake of profits. No mission agency serving Jesus must ever be mean, but it must always be lean. Wasn't that what Jesus taught his disciples? Their support and supplies were marginal at best. Basically, they lived off the land one day at a time.

The apostle Paul was so concerned, lest he get fat in the ministry, that he worked his way across Asia and into Europe. He didn't have to do this, he said, because he was entitled to material returns for spiritual ministry. But avoiding at all costs the charge that he was in it for the money, he never sponged off anyone.

But now our agencies flourish in an era of unprecedented wealth and prosperity. Never in history have so many Christians had so much money to give, and so much freedom to support, so many missionaries.

But prosperity brings its own temptations. Just ask King Hezekiah, one of the few godly kings of Judah, who succumbed to wealth and flaunted it before the pagans he had invited to his palace.

I'm not saying we have to live on the edge, with only two bullets and six gallons of gasoline. But to be effective in winning spiritual battles, we must be much more disciplined in using our wealth than we are now. The unbelieving world sees our wealth as a stumbling block.

Protestants generally have lost touch with the incredible leanness, poverty, and suffering that have marked the history of world missions. Used to dealing with hundreds of millions of dollars, we expect that missionaries should receive about the same comfort margins as the rest of us.

On the other hand, Capt. McCampbell returned safely, mission accomplished, with little to spare. It was enough. That's the faith goal of our mission—enough to carry out God's assignment—no more and no less.

It would be wise, and biblical, for us to husband our resources, use them sparingly for carefully defined purposes, and refrain from lavishing our larder around the world for a lot of projects that could be better handled for less money by the Christians already there. Prosperity in this world does not last forever. If we're not careful, we may run out of bullets and gasoline before our battle is over.

Trading combat boots
for sneakers

The approach into Colorado Springs airport last month took me over familiar terrain—the scoured ravines and scrubby vegetation of the Army's base at Fort Carson. I say familiar because that's where I took my basic military training to prepare for combat in Korea, which, incidentally, I never saw.

That's another story. This story is about cold, dust, marching, cleaning rifles, boots, pots and pans, and barracks, and finding out first-hand why the mountains are called Rocky. Basic training was always expected to be rough and tough ever since Valley Forge, I guess.

No more. Army, Navy, and Air Force are under increasing pressure to stem a high dropout rate among trainees. The answer? Make it easier for everyone. The obstacle course at Fort Carson still makes me tremble, but now the Army says trainees can run around, instead of over, some walls.

Of course, not everyone is delighted at the sight of soldiers-to-be swapping combat boots for sneakers, and running at their own pace instead of in formation. We won't know the outcomes of this new approach to "basic" until soldiers are battle tested. Quite possibly, we could be lowering the dropout rate of trainees at the expense of losing a war.

Our churches face the same dilemma when it comes to basic training for combat in God's world mission. How tough shall we make it for someone who volunteers to serve Jesus in a hostile environment? How much "basic" shall we require for spiritual warfare?

Should we really worry about the risk of making "basic" too tough, lest a volunteer decide to go somewhere else?

I hope we don't take a cue from the military. I hope we don't trade combat boots for sneakers. What do we really gain by making it easier to serve Jesus on the front lines in enemy territory? Nothing. But we lose a lot. If we don't require rough and tough preparation for war, our casualties will mount and we will not gain new ground for God's kingdom.

As I have reviewed the training of numerous would-be missionaries, some of their accounts reminded me of the children of Europe who were sent off to battle in the Crusades. I refer not to their passing academic credentials, but to their lack of battle testedness in the U.S. Sticking out like one of those Fort Carson rocks I had to sleep on was the notable absence of any significant engagements with pagans.

This kind of "basic" cannot be built into a curriculum. It must be accepted voluntarily by the wise person who understands the rough-and-tumble life of a soldier of Jesus in enemy territory. It begins by encountering the unbelieving world in teenage and college years. For many, it continues by engaging peers in business and professional life, before trying to be a "tentmaker" overseas.

"Katy, bar the door" I say to those who would send anyone anywhere without significant battle scars. We must fight spiritual warfare with the best trained, most experienced women and men we can find. Our churches and mission agencies must discount the risk of losing potential recruits in favor of choosing and sending people who know the difference between combat boots and sneakers.

Wanted: urban missionary Rambos

Pith helmets vanished with hula hoops, but what's the new missionary trademark: a laptop computer, a VCR, an Izod sports shirt? Probably none of the above, because today's composite missionary is as remarkably diverse as urban Chicago's ethnic makeup. Remote jungle missionaries continue to attack the frontiers of darkness, of course, but since the Auca massacre in 1956 their prominence in missions has steadily diminished.

However, nothing has arisen to replace this image, despite the act that the mission field itself—the vast unreached world—has shifted like a crunching, incinerating mass of molten lava, overwhelming the world's cities. You think New York City is jammed? A mere 11,480 people per square mile live there. But in Hong Kong, for example, 247,500 people pack a square mile.

The prognosis for the future staggers not only economists and politicians, but also church and missions leaders. Reports the Population Crisis Committee: "By the end of this century, the urban population of the developing (poor) world will be almost double the size of that of the industrialized (rich) world." Some scholars say that every day a quarter of a million people flock into the world's cities.

Statistics by themselves do not sharpen the Christian public's perceptions of the missionary's role. People need another "pith helmet" image to grasp what it's like to be an urban missionary. A friend of ours tried his best in this letter:

"Our problem is not the terrible smog, it's the moral decline around our meeting place. We see the effects of drug culture. The nearby bar is owned by pushers. Others live in our courtyard and stash drugs and money just outside our entrance. Addicts high on drugs defecate in the stairwell at our entrance. Children playing in the courtyard have to avoid discarded syringes. Major police invasions, patrols, and searches have put several pushers out of circulation, but others come to take their place."

In our frustration and impatience we might wish that Rambo would become our new missionary image. The reality, however, is that we don't recruit Rambos and send them to the world's cities, with guns blazing, to clean out the gangs and drug pushers. What do we do? At home, we flee such terrible neighborhoods; yet in our suburban and rural churches, we plead for young people to leave their sterilized environments and plunge into the world's highly infected cities for the sake of Christ.

On the whole, as churches and mission agencies we have not adequately faced the world's massive population swing away from rural to urban areas. Notable exceptions notwithstanding, we have not been able to ignite much enthusiasm for urban missions.

Not only is recruiting tough, but fund raising for urban work is like pulling rusty nails from old lumber. When the workers do get there, they struggle to find apartments and agonize about both air pollution and social pollution. They write home and hope that their supporters have at last some glimmer of understanding about what it takes to build friendships among city-dwellers. When converts do not pour in like crowds cramming into a rock concert, the home offices and churches wonder if such resistant fields are worth the time, suffering, and money.

Therefore, the urban missionary's image often quickly melts away in the melange of other mission work. Urban workers are swallowed up in the Christian public's consciousness at home like the millions of peasants somehow dissolving into the bowels of Manila, Cairo, and Nairobi.

Perhaps Rambo is the answer after all. Not the guns-blazing Rambo of film fame, but a consciousness-raising Rambo in the home office and in the church who will be able to chart a new course and carve a new image to reflect the most monumental worldwide change in missions history—the migration of millions from rural to urban jungles.

What do "the best" look like?

One of the pleasures, and risks, of writing a column is that you'll run into someone who has read it and then asks you what you mean. A couple of weeks ago, one of our ushers, a young man headed for the mission field, handed me a bulletin and asked: "You keep saying we should send only the best to the field."

Caught off guard, I said, "Yes, that's right. I guess I mean they should be . . ." As I sat down in church, I thought I had to answer his question more fully. I hope he reads this column.

Number one, spiritual maturity and experience. The best know what it's like to walk with God, hunger for him more than anything else, and help people to know him. As spiritually disciplined people, they are faithful in prayer, Bible meditation, and serious study of the Scripture. They've gotten beyond the ABCs. They are making a significant contribution to the worship, fellowship, and witness of their church. They know how to give.

The best have learned how to swim with the sharks. They have exploded out of the evangelical ghetto to seriously engage pagans. After they have memorized their Bible and theology outlines, they have thrown these truths, and their lives, to the sharks and lived to tell about it.

Roll up their sleeves and you'll find the tattoo of spiritual leadership. They stand tall; they aim high. They can honestly attest, as Ezra the scribe did, that God's good hand is upon them. They smell of Jesus.

They've been knocked down a couple of times and have scars to prove it. They have discovered "beauty for ashes, the oil of joy for mourning, the garment of praise for the spirit of heaviness." The best really are "trees of righteousness, the planting of the Lord."

The best see Jesus in the multitudes—"inasmuch as you have done it to the least of these"—and they see the multitudes through his eyes. They don't begrudge listening to someone for a couple of hours over a cup of coffee. Somehow, like incessant waves of the sea, hurting people find their way to the best and receive tender care for their wounds. The best are drained for Jesus.

The best lust for the culture—books, food, politics, economics, music, habits, customs, religion, history—of the people they want to go to. Like a nest full of freshly hatched robins, the best gorge themselves on everything foreign. In the U.S. they find the urban ethnic neighborhood of their adopted country, and walk the streets, smell the smells, observe the habits, sit in the cafes, eat the food, and worship in the churches. They go to the campus and make friends with students from that country.

The best know that the church is the only game in town. They don't run it, they serve it. They realize that "parachurch" is an anomaly of history that does not entitle them to ignore or abuse God's people who comprise his church, Christ's body.

The best have cultivated satisfying levels of integrity, respect, and intimacy in their marriages. They nurture and encourage each other to be the best. They strive for transparency about money, power, and sex. If single, they have wrestled through their singleness vis-à-vis God's loving, wise plan for their lives. They do not see singleness as "second best," nor are they consumed by a craving for a mate.

When the best apply for service, they do not ask what the mission board can do for them, but what they can do for the mission. They are team players, not prima donnas. The best aspire to be professionals, just like surgeons and scientists, and they never stop trying to improve.

The best will have done serious study in missions, Bible, theology, anthropology, and cross-cultural communications. They know the value of mining the rich storehouse of the accumulated spiritual and practical wisdom of their predecessors.

"Lord, send us many more like the young man I met who wants to be only the very best for you."

Where are the pioneers?

Remember what your parents gave you on your **tenth birthday?** I don't either, but I know they did not buy two pages in the country's newspapers to tell the world I was 10 years old. But that's what Apple did for its Macintosh computers last month. Hard to believe that the computer that cranks out these columns twice a month has been alive for only 10 years. Even harder to believe, it's obsolete in the exploding world of computer technology. In computer exploration you have to be a pioneer every six months or so.

However, in world missions it seems as if our pioneers only come around every 100 years or so. We don't have to create missions innovations every six months, but more than once a century would not be asking too much.

Our reviews of missions history usually focus on the breakthroughs that came after William Carey. We cover such giants as Hudson Taylor, John R. Mott, Rowland Bingham, A.B. Simpson, and Robert E. Speer, but we usually forget Lottie Moon, Mary Slessor, and Amy Carmichael, among others.

Probably our greatest explosion of missionary pioneers occurred shortly after World War II, although before the war we were blessed with Cameron Townsend (Wycliffe Bible Translators, 1934), Clarence Jones (World Radio Missionary Fellowship, 1931), Dawson Trotman (The Navigators, 1933), and Joy Ridderhof (Gospel Recordings, 1939). After the war God gave us Robert Evans (Greater Europe Mission, 1949) and Philip Armstrong (SEND International, 1947), as well as Bill Bright (Campus Crusade, 1951), George Verwer (Operation Mobilization, 1958), Loren Cunningham (Youth With A Mission, 1960), and Brother Andrew (Open Doors, 1973).

But as we approach the year 2000, have we run out of pioneers? Where do we find our new pioneers for world evangelization? Is there still room for pioneers, or do our mission structures stifle them? I'm not thinking so much of the missionary who begins a new work in a Hong Kong high rise, or with an unreached tribe in Zaire, but of the person who launches a Macintosh-like innovation that forever changes how we do our work. Clarence Jones started a radio station, George Verwer launched a ship, Bill Bright produced a movie (the Jesus film), and Dawson Trotman taught people how to do one-on-one discipleship.

Going back to computers, I'm fascinated by the story of Bill Gates of Microsoft, a pioneer in the industry. Gates, gripped by an idea when he was still a Harvard undergraduate, went on to surpass giant IBM. As Christians trying to storm the strongholds of unbelief and build the church around the world, what can we do to produce a Bill Gates for world missions?

Some would answer that we can't make pioneers, only God can. Ultimately, of course, that is true, but God grows pioneers in certain soils, and I'm wondering if our church, mission, and scholastic soils are encouraging or discouraging the germination of pioneers for the next century. God took Dawson Trotman off the streets of Los Angeles, and Bill Bright out of the business world, both unlikely soils for future missions pioneers. But God also used friends and churches to get these men headed in the right direction, and to pursue their visions and dreams.

Perhaps American culture, religious and otherwise,

militates against pioneers. Perhaps our missions culture squelches them. Perhaps our churches and schools weed out those who seem to march to a different drummer.

I hope I am mistaken. But if I am right, then we must get on our faces before God and beseech him to do for our generation what Joel prophesied. We desperately need young women and men—not just Americans, either—who will dream big dreams, and obey the vision God gives them, so that the world of missions will be set aflame.

The Task Force

A "knowledge gap"
crying to be bridged

A couple of weeks ago I held forth on a national call-in radio program as the missions expert. After a brief introduction by the show's host, I took a deep breath and waited for the switchboard to light up. I also prayed that God would keep me from saying something stupid.

Feeling like one of those little ducks that used to waddle across the firing line in a shooting gallery, I had no idea what was on the minds of America's Christians, but since the Gulf War had already erupted, I anticipated some questions about missions in the Middle East. One caller criticized missionaries who had come home, calling them "chicken," but he was adequately handled by subsequent callers who rose to defend them. This was early in the show, and I hoped his call and the ensuing debate would not set the tone for the whole hour.

I was relieved when it didn't, but unprepared for and surprised by the majority of the calls. Most of the people wanted to know how to do something for God in world missions. I have no idea what churches these people attended, but it was abundantly clear that they were seeking advice about how to get started. They spoke from a variety of professional and educational experiences. They told me what they were doing and asked if I knew of any mission board, or any needs, where they might fit.

They surprised me, because I was expecting more general, or theoretical questions. I was unprepared, because I don't carry a missionary "help wanted" list in my hip pocket. I could encourage them generally, but not specifically.

The upbeat side is that there seems to be a huge reservoir of good will, of positive attitudes toward missionary service, across the country. Christians do want to make their lives count for God. Missionary work attracts them. These callers were not Bible college or seminary students; they were already following a career path, but they recognized a need to change direction.

It's important to remember this, lest we fall into despair and make false generalizations about the attitudes of people in our churches about world missions. These are people to be cultivated and encouraged, not whipsawed.

The downside is that, for all their good intentions people looking for a missionary vocation don't know where to turn. They are like tourists standing on the South Rim of the Grand Canyon trying to yell across to National Park Service people on the North Rim. Nothing there but emptiness.

I'm talking about simple, basic information. Perhaps all of our promotion—verbal, printed, visual—goes right over their heads. Perhaps the experts are talking to themselves about issues and trends in missions that the average Christian doesn't know or care about. The missions "knowledge gap" must be bridged by some new kinds of communications strategies and tools.

Our country has raced to close all kinds of sophisticated "gaps" and our missions have tried valiantly to stay current with new strategies and emphases. Meanwhile, I wonder if we've left our troops behind, wandering in the desert and looking for a place to get into the battle for the souls of women and men. Somehow, we have to link up with these good-hearted people—most of them, I think, far away from the citadels of mission studies, and offer them a helping hand. Not more sophisticated research and seminars, but the simple ABCs.

God is in the fly

The speaker commanded my attention, but not half **as effectively as the fly buzzing around the bald head of the frustrated fellow sitting in front of me.** Helpless to relieve the man's pestiferous annoyance, I watched the cycle of landing, crawling, and taking off in rhythm with the victim's angry but futile swipes.

How like God, who keeps landing on our bald heads, as it were, to get our attention. He will not let us go, no matter how far we run to escape the implications of his salvation offered to the world in his Son. God is the great disturber, the supreme troubler, buzzing at the wicked and righteous alike.

We may sometimes swipe at God out of deliberate disobedience. We hear or read something that momentarily nudges us to follow the Lord. But we quickly dismiss the thought simply as an emotional reaction and keep on drifting.

Sometimes we try to drive away the Holy Spirit's nudging by indulging more furiously in our personal agenda. Certainly, we do not lack for good things to do and good causes to support. But they may not align with Jesus' command to spread the good news about his death, resurrection, and return. We can't focus on the right priorities, so we keep chasing flies away.

Meanwhile, our pesky God keeps bothering us. That's his job, because it promotes his glory, our godliness, and the growth of his kingdom. He will not let us get away with routinely praying, "Thy kingdom come," and doing nothing about it. He won't let us sing, "Jesus loves the little children," without lifting a hand to help.

God sent a great fish to swallow Jonah when he ran away. Jonah finally saw the senselessness of trying to outrun God, so he preached and Nineveh repented. Taking another swipe at God, Jonah said, "I told you so. I knew it all the time. That's why I ran away."

In his anger, Jonah asked God to take his life, but God gave him shade from the heat. Jonah was learning that God cannot be so summarily dismissed. God's fly kept buzzing, only this time it took the form of a worm that attacked and killed Jonah's shady plant. Jonah got mad enough to die.

God then drove a stake in Jonah's heart. "Jonah, you feel sorry for losing your shady plant, but you feel no sorrow for Nineveh," he said. "I feel sorry for 120,000 innocent children in the city."

Thank God for all the miraculous plants he grows for our nourishment and care. We don't deserve them, of course. But what stumbling blocks they become when they stifle our compassion for those who do not love and worship the one true God through his Son. While we enjoy our shade, others suffer the consequences of sin and separation from God. Therefore, God sends his flies, or worms, to disturb us and to expose what's really first in our hearts—shade trees or lost people.

God did not quit on Jonah, and he will not quit on us. How fortunate we are to know God's big picture program. We know he wants to conform us to Jesus, to be his people in society, to be faithful in using everything he gives us to love the Ninevehs of our world. We know he seeks people to worship him now and to join the heavenly throng of worshippers of Jesus. We know Jesus calls his church to be faithful witnesses to him.

Therefore, when God's flies buzz around us, and around our churches, be careful about chasing them away. If we do, we may be disregarding something God wants to tell us.

"My bones are too old"

Begged by her grandson one day to get down on the **floor and play with him, my sister-in-law had to decline.** "Why not, grandma?" he asked. "Because my bones are too old," she explained. Looking hopefully to the future, he asked her, "Will they get better?"

Traveling the church missionary conference circuit this past winter, I've been asked the same question—not about my bones, but about mission boards: "Will they get better?" Asked not by critics but by godly, concerned, praying, sacrificially giving friends of missionaries. They wonder if the boards can't play anymore because their bones are too old.

They have lived long enough, and heard enough missionary candidates, and read enough missionary prayer letters, to know that something is amiss. Most of them grew up with people who became missionaries after World War II. They have supported them for a long time.

But now they are standing up like groundhogs on the edge of a cornfield, carefully scanning the horizon for signs of change, and yes, possible danger, too. They feel that mission boards have not kept pace with the times. They have been too slow to change, too slow to recognize significant changes in people's lives, in their churches, in education, in jobs at home, in economics, in world religions, in management techniques, and in international business and communications.

One question starkly nails the issue: "Why are missions still operating in the 1890s?" Mission boards may deny this, but they must take their supporters' perceptions seriously. It won't do to say, "Aw, that's not true." I've looked for some basic causes of this perception, and would like to suggest a few.

Some boards take their friends—individuals and churches—for granted. They do not keep their corporate ears to the ground. They don't say "thank you" often enough. Missionary prayer letters arrive far too infrequently, and don't say much when they do. In a day when business has learned the hard way that consumers must be served, too many boards neglect their friends. They practice little partnership, happily receiving for years on end but rarely ministering. Smallish churches especially notice this benign neglect.

Our friends see mission board duplication and overlap at home and abroad, and relatively little cooperation and cost-saving. "Why can't they get together?" they often ask. Many people in the pews have neither time nor patience to sort out the multitude of organizational, doctrinal, and traditional nuances that separate boards. They think that if the boards really put their heads together, they could manage world evangelization much more efficiently. They love to see specific targets being met in the unreached world, but find it hard to justify planting 57 varieties of churches in the same tomato patch.

One sore point pops up like a boil on the back of the neck: "Why do missionaries cost so much?" This comes from our friends who need two incomes, and a little more, to survive. They are living on the edge economically and are appalled by some support needs. Mission boards, they think, have been much too slow to recognize this collision and therefore should back off and reconsider.

Our friends sense a lack of supervision and pastoral care of their missionaries on the field. Too late, they hear about their wounded missionaries and wonder if the boards could not do much more to help them through their struggles. Too many times they feel like they're trying to crack the CIA when they try to get answers from the boards about their missionaries' problems.

Will "the old bones get better?" Some brittle boards may snap, but others are already changing. The critical issue now is to listen.

On the right plane?

The plane was packed. Last-minute travelers laden with bags trundled down the aisle. The man stopped and checked his boarding pass for his and his wife's assigned seats: 22 E and F, the row in front of us. Sure enough, they were occupied and the people said, yes, they were in the right seats.

No fight ensued. I was pleasantly surprised how amiable the fellow was. "Just glad to be on the plane," he said to no one in particular. To his wife he said, "Don't worry. They'll find us some seats." And they did, a couple of rows behind us.

Not long afterward the man discovered why seats 22 E and F had been taken. No, it wasn't a computer foul-up. He and his wife had dashed down the wrong jetway. Gates B12 and 13 opened side by side in Terminal 4 of the Phoenix Skyharbor airport. One led to Chicago, the other to Dallas. They thought they were headed for Dallas, but now climbing to 31,000 feet over the Sonora Desert they discovered that Chicago was their destination.

Were they sincere? Yes. Were they dedicated? Yes. Were they zealous? Yes. Did they have the right motives? Yes. Did they have their "support"? Yes, they had their tickets in hand. Were they on the right plane? No. Unfortunately, in our missionary zeal we sometimes take the wrong planes. No amount of zeal and dedication will make up for a lack of knowledge, wisdom, and understanding about Scripture, culture, and the church. Such knowledge is critical, however, because many gates and flights beckon us like a shimmering mirage in the desert.

Mission ministries and needs, no matter how attractive and appealing, can be seductive and carnal when they stress how easy it is to win people to faith in Christ, and how exciting it is to be part of something big God is doing (as if God never does small things).

Every day planes lift off from our American runways carrying eager, zealous people, who depart with high hopes, expectations, and steep price tags. But just because they are on the plane does not mean they will necessarily achieve their expectations, or do God's will. They could very well be flying in the wrong direction, for a number of reasons.

Poor motives. Their missionary engines have been revved up by the Go! motive. Or, they see themselves as the answer to other people's needs. They may be overcome by pity. They may be driven to impart superior ways.

Misunderstandings. Of themselves, their strengths, their weaknesses. Of their partnership with the church. Of the nature of the battle that awaits them. Of culture, language. Of their own cultural baggage.

Spiritual immaturity. They've taken the required courses, but have no battle ribbons to show they have previously encountered some pagans. They are bottle fed, and have not yet mastered the knack of feeding themselves.

Theological shallowness. Their theological roots have not penetrated beyond some proof texts. They have never been challenged by pluralism and syncretism, or by Islam, Hinduism, and Buddhism.

Should we then ground them for awhile? Perhaps. The sheer number of Christian bodies being transported abroad does not necessarily prove we are pushing back the kingdom of darkness. Rather than rushing to go, and running through the wrong gate to the wrong plane, perhaps we should first check the integrity and biblical values of both our missionary appeals and our responses.

God places no premium on either our cleverness to sell ministries and needs, or on our speedy responses. He does require honesty, compassion, and justice. Jesus Christ builds his church his way. Before we reserve our seats to do his work in the world, we must master his priorities and values.

Our newest missionaries

Last night we commissioned Greg and Debby to be our newest missionaries, the 319th and 320th on our support roll since 1885.** I tell this story because there's a lot of negative stuff going around about the local church and world missions. Unfortunately, some of it is true. Virtually every week I hear grim stories about churches reducing their missions budgets and about missionaries coming home (or not being able to go in the first place) because they lack financial support.

So, we make no apology for disrupting the comfort zones of many Christians and local churches who are sleeping through unparalleled opportunities to invest their lives and money in the most demanding and the most satisfying cause of all, Christ's Great Commission.

On the other hand, Greg and Debby prove a number of things we need to recall. One is that God has not quit calling people to commit themselves to missionary careers. He kicked Paul and Barnabas out of a cozy place in the church at Antioch almost 2,000 years ago, and the Holy Spirit, the great disturber of Christians, continues to burn missionary zeal into the hearts of people today.

Too easily we trash the baby boomers and baby busters, consigning them to the pits of self-gratification, forgetting that God's commitment to world evangelization drives him to keep on rescuing people from their own plans and giving them something far superior to do. We can join God's drive for missionaries by giving people like Greg and Debby a platform in our churches. The kids coming along in school and college must be confronted by alternative career role models.

Commissioning Greg and Debby confirmed a deep

theological conviction that millions of people are hopelessly lost unless they welcome Jesus Christ as Lord and Savior. Why send Greg and Debby to suffer through language learning, lower living standards, separation from friends and family, and the painful adjustment to a foreign culture unless we believe the compelling biblical mandate to find and rescue the lost sheep?

Of course, theological fifth columns have betrayed the gospel and Jesus Christ's unique role as Savior of the world almost from day one. Great waves of evangelism and mission have vanished like streaking meteors. Once-flourishing missions programs have sputtered and died because, in effect, theologians decided that people of all faiths would be saved if they held to the truths of their religions.

No, syncretism and universalism have not died, but neither has the same New Testament fervor that compelled the apostle Paul to confess that he himself lived under a divinely imposed debt to the pagan world. The apostle's sense of urgency and sacrifice still captures the hearts of young women and men.

Last night we not only commissioned Greg and Debby, we committed ourselves to a partnership as critical as that between mother and newborn baby. We're proud they represent us, our church, our convictions, our missionary impulse. How well they fulfill their dreams and calling will depend in large part on how well we nourish and cherish them. Their spiritual prosperity will depend in large degree on how much we invest in praying, first for their own faith race with Jesus Christ—for their own growth and integrity—and second for their success in teaching and telling people about Jesus Christ.

Woe to the church that gives up on her youth, her baby boomers and baby busters. Woe to the church that quits believing that middle-aged professionals and retired businessmen can be struck down and raised up like the apostle Paul was to tramp the world for Jesus. Woe to the church that stamps out the fires of passion for lost souls, that consigns Jesus Christ to the same level as Moses, Buddha, Krishna, and Muhammad. Woe to the church that sends out missionaries but forgets to feed their spirits as well as their support accounts. As Jesus himself solemnly warned, woe to the church that has a name for being alive, but is dead.

Pastor John, Steve, and Judy

The wind ripped across the country graveyard, not sure if it was the last gasp of winter or the herald of spring. The rolling Pennsylvania farmland stood barren, as if awaiting its wake-up call to produce another year's crops. Into that soil we lowered the casket of Pastor John, 82.

I recalled the words of Jesus, "Unless a grain of wheat falls into the earth and dies, it remains alone; but if it dies, it bears much fruit."

Some of Pastor John's fruit huddled around his grave—not just his physical fruit but his spiritual fruit as well. He had borne much fruit, not only in his founding and building up of a vibrant church, but in his worldwide vision which he energetically pursued to the end. World missions was a joyful watchword of his lifetime, not a grudging adjunct of the church's program. He was vital and alert to the end, always curious to know how his missionaries were doing and what God was up to in the world at large.

As we drifted away from the cemetery, I pondered the future. This was a time not only to mourn Pastor John but to wonder if the next generation of pastors would fan the flames of world evangelization as he had done.

God gladdened my heart with the recollection of Steve and Judy. The night before, we had gone beyond our usual bedtime to bask in their enthusiasm for their new venture in world missions. Steve and Judy's parents had been nurtured in Pastor John's church. Steve and Judy had grown up breathing the air of missions in junior church, Sunday school, youth groups, camps, and the worship services. Their parents respected and loved missionaries who had grown up in their church.

Steve and Judy are the fruit of Pastor John's heart for missions. He had seen to it that world missions was more than an annual conference, more than checks sent off to unknown people. Pastor John's church grew its own missionaries, not just for one generation, but for a second represented by Steve and Judy.

The earth had reclaimed one of the Lord's own that day, but his fruit would go on, not just in the church, but around the globe. Sons and daughters of Pastor John's church are serving Jesus Christ in Asia, Africa, the Middle East, Europe, Latin America, and North America.

All of this happened without the razzle-dazzle that so often passes for missions today, without unseemly pressure, without the gimmicks we so often think are needed to get people interested in world missions. It happened because Pastor John set the pace, set the tone, impregnated the whole place with missions thinking and passion. It happened because missions thinking, praying, giving, and going were rooted firmly in Scripture and in the faithful missionary exposition of God's word.

Consequently, his church produced the two things missions leaders are most fearful of losing today: candidates and support. His church produced the two things missionaries need more than anything else: tons of love and prayer.

Where does it all begin? With a pastor who is willing to turn his life and ministry into a grain of wheat, to fall into the earth and die. Such pastors don't have to be dragged kicking and screaming into world missions support. They will have a vision and a passion for the mission fields of the world that will outlast their sermons and extend the name of Christ worldwide through succeeding generations of sons and daughters of the church.

The local church must be the seedbed of all that we hope to achieve in obedience to Christ's missionary command. If we don't see more people like Pastor John filling our pulpits in the future, then the outlook for world evangelization is bleak. But if we do see more like him, then we need not be panicked into all sorts of artificial respiration for the missions enterprise.

Remember the *Zam Zam*?

The **"Titanic" did not sink at the box office.** During the film's production it was ridiculed as an over-budget, floating disaster. But when the votes were in, "Titanic" won a record-tying 11 Oscars. It ranks as Hollywood's most expensive movie and all-time box-office hit. News reports tell of a growing addiction to seeing the movie.

Many conversations in our area sooner or later get around to this: "Have you seen 'Titanic'?" If you haven't you usually get a lecture to go see it right away. If you have, well then you have something to talk about.

One way to steer the conversation away from your embarrassment at not having seen "Titanic" is to ask, "Do you remember the *Zam Zam*?" Now the shoe is on the other foot. "The *Zam Zam*. What's that?" For sure, the *Zam Zam* doesn't stick in our minds like the *Titanic* and Pearl Harbor.

However, in the annals of missionary heroism, the sinking of the *Zam Zam* in the spring of 1941 off the coast of South Africa will be long remembered. The story is equally as gripping as that of the *Titanic*. Originally a British vessel, the *Zam Zam* was sold to an Egyptian company. The steamship sailed from New York with a passenger list that included 140 missionaries bound for various mission fields in Africa. Thinking the *Zam Zam* was a British troopship, the Germans sank it. When they discovered their mistake, the Germans rescued everybody. Not a single missionary died, but of course, they lost all their possessions. A *Life* magazine photographer on board took remarkable photos of the disaster, which stirred England and the U.S.

While millions of people watch the tragic loss of life among the passengers of the *Titanic*, relatively few remember the cost of obedience to the orders of Jesus to spread the good news about him among all nations. Even church members tend to forget that they are all called to pay extraordinarily high prices for obedience. Perhaps that's because we've made entrance into the Lord's army a relatively easy, comfortable commitment. We forget the church exists for mission.

Once in a while we get stiff reminders of the cost of commitment, as when the *Zam Zam* goes down, or when five young American men are speared to death in the jungles of Ecuador. Of course, some critics write such things off as a tragic waste. But those who take the words of Jesus seriously soon realize that the best thing in life is to lose your life for him.

Conceivably, we can use the *Titanic* as a warning of what can happen to even the world's best engineering plans. Or as a warning to the rich and famous that the good times often come to a disastrous conclusion. On the other hand, the *Zam Zam* reminds us of the priceless heritage we have in the church, because thousands of missionaries have been willing to lay their lives on the line for Jesus.

The sinking of the *Zam Zam* also forces us to ask the current generation of would-be followers of Christ how much they are willing to risk for Jesus. Of course, in God's economy the so-called "losses" add up to incalculable riches in his kingdom.

Most people, if they had a choice, would prefer to sail amid the luxuries of the *Titanic* rather than on a nondescript, slow Egyptian vessel. That choice reflects our values in a nutshell. Unless Christians get their choices and values in line with those of Jesus, we may lose the engagement with the powers of darkness and unbelief that stand in the way of bringing people to know Christ's love and forgiveness.

Smaller! Are you crazy?

Once upon a time the ministry's area directors, vice-presidents, managers, and fund raisers **rushed to their CEO and cried, "John, there's another ministry started right in our territory, and it's going like gang busters.** In fact, they're making a lot more converts than we are. What are we going to do? This is a *kairos* moment! If we don't come up with some new strategies—perhaps even a paradigm shift—we're sunk."

And John said, "Praise the Lord! That's okay, guys. As their work gets bigger, ours will have to get smaller." John said those words with perfect joy (John 3:29, 30).

Unlike John, we are so stingy when it comes to rejoicing with those who rejoice. I don't hear much joy in the camp when a new work comes along and steals our thunder. Rather, we self-defensively crawl back into our HQs and plot some way to outdo the other ministry, so we don't lose our workers and supporters.

Why not? It's the good old competitive American way of doing business. If your competitor builds a better mouse trap, send in a spy to steal his secrets, unleash an advertising blitz, or, better yet, hire his CEO. If that fails, launch an unfriendly takeover bid. United Airlines finally got a nonstop route from Chicago to London, and trumpeted the news with double-page newspaper spreads. American Airlines fired back and said, in effect,

"That's nothing. We have three daily nonstops to London."

Are things really that bad in Christian ministries? Not quite, but almost. Some justify our mission competition by pointing to the results, as if they atone for all ungodly attitudes and practices. Leaders cringe when anyone suggests that perhaps it is time to "grow less," as John put it. That's fatal, they say, because our public would never stand for it.

Such self-justification flies in the face of the biblical principle that, with God, less is more. He doesn't need bigness. He doesn't need organizations to grow greater. He is looking for smallness that generates faith and total dependency on him. He looks for a few Gideons who will abandon themselves to him. God cannot stand pride, and nothing panders to pride quite like bigness.

John was big and he had to become smaller and smaller and smaller, for the sake of the Lord Jesus Christ. He had to cash in at the pinnacle of his popularity. That was painful for John and his followers, but he understood God's time and God's plan.

God picked John for a very strategic ministry, preparing the public for the arrival of Jesus. When it was over, John had enough sense to back away. Competition fled his spirit faster than the flicker of a bird's wing.

Wouldn't it be wonderful, a friend wrote me, if our mission agencies would say something honest like: "We're not doing a very good job, but we're trying to do the best we can with what we've got." Mission agencies somehow choke on the fact that people hunger for honesty, transparency, vulnerability, and integrity the way some of us salivate for Chicago deep-dish pizza. They fear telling us about their problems, their mistakes, and their disasters because they fear losing their bigness. They can't bear to say, "That's okay, guys. This hurts, but we're going to get smaller so we can get better."

Instead, the usual spin goes something like this: "Yes, we know those other guys are there, and they're doing a good work, but they're not our kind of guys, and besides, we're going to do it a lot better." Our churches are long overdue for a refreshing breeze of John-style humility. Down with self-aggrandizement. It has no place in God's work.

SRO for missionaries?

Last night, 150,000 people packed Chicago's Grant Park to hear Placido Domingo, who, said the *Chicago Tribune*'s music critic, "sounded for all the world like a million pesetas."** Music is big, not just in the summer and not just for the general public. Churches have learned that a concert is one sure-fire way to get a crowd. Music pulls 'em in like nothing else. Music beats preaching every time; music beats missionaries every time.

I heard a local radio station plug a Christian concert. The event was sure to be a sellout, the announcer warned, so get your tickets early. I wondered how long it's been—indeed, if ever—that a church hung out the SRO (standing room only) sign for a visiting missionary.

Compared to musicians, why are missionaries as attractive as bees at your backyard barbecue? Oh, that's easy, you say. Music draws young people; that's who these performances are supposed to bring in. That's how you expose non-Christian kids to the gospel.

Fair enough, I say, but why do we stay home when our missionaries and overseas church leaders come to town? Very simply, our culture has changed our habits. Our old habits told us that if our church was open for a meeting, we'd be there whatever night of the week it was, regardless of who was preaching. Our new habits tell us that a meeting at church represents just one of many choices, and very often the missionary speaker ranks last.

People choose what they're "sold." Music is an easy sell; missions is a hard sell. Music doesn't require much promotion; missions does. Music has a much broader base to draw on. The pool of potential listeners is far greater, because missionaries do not have as many fans as Michael Card does.

If we ever hang out the SRO sign for missionaries, it will be because the church's leaders have decided to sell missions, not just to the faithful but to the people who don't know any missionaries, and don't want to. People take their cues from what they see up front. If they see the senior pastor and youth pastor, for example, pull out all the stops for a missionary speaker—with the same enthusiasm they generate for a concert—they'll begin to think, "Hey, this must be important." Otherwise, it's a yawner.

The pastoral staff and missions committee will not only promote, they will plan and package their missionaries for maximum exposure. Unfortunately, I've been to missions conferences and found the youth off somewhere on retreat. That is inappropriate planning.

But we can't stop at selling. Our culture also dictates that we package programs for maximum appeal. So, when our people scan their choices, they'll say, "Wow!

That's got some pop and sizzle. I think we'll go to that."
Otherwise, they'll probably groan and say, "Oh, no, not
another missionary."

Appropriate packaging begins well in advance. It includes consistent, informative, attractive publicity. The
missionary has to be sold as the main event, to be sure,
but people also need to be sold on benefits. That's the
cardinal rule of promotion. Yes, Christians do ask,
"What's in it for me? Why should I take an hour to hear
about an unknown person from an obscure part of the
world that I don't care about?" Why should they?

We have to know the cultural pounding our people
are taking. We have to adjust to why they choose to
spend their time as they do. We have to grasp their values and attitudes, find out what's behind their choices.
We must keep on banging away at their minds and
hearts about why it's important to get in step with God's
missionary heart and commitment.

Maybe missionaries will never draw SRO crowds, but
every church that says it's a biblical church better bust a
gut trying.

Stop, look, and listen

One night, after a day of trout fishing, I was sleeping very soundly in an old cabin in the mountains of Pennsylvania. Suddenly, I was jolted by what
seemed to be an earthquake. The ground trembled, the
cabin rattled, my bunk bounced, and I quaked. From
out of nowhere in the dark of night a freight train thundered through the valley.

The rusty old black and white sign at the nearby

grade crossing warned me to Stop, Look, and Listen. But except for school bus drivers, hardly anyone pays attention to the warning signs. Life is too fast, and we're too much in a hurry, to stop, look, and listen.

I wonder if the same could be said of our churches. I have churches in mind here more than individuals. We have seriously cultivated the idea that each believer should listen to God, find his will, and do it. We have not invested so much of our energy in finding out what the church—the body of believers— should be doing.

For example, Mr. and Mrs. Jones stop, look, and listen to God. He tells them he wants them to serve him in Uzbekistan. They go to their church and say, "God has spoken to us. We believe he wants us to serve him in Uzbekistan. Will you send us, pray for us, and support us?"

The board of missions, the elders, the pastor, or whoever replies, "Well, we'll have to think about that. You know, we're pretty heavily committed already, and we don't know if we can afford to support any more missionaries. Our giving is off a little this year, and we're trying to get the building fund off the ground."

Who is listening to God? Why should the initiative for missions rest primarily with individuals rather than the church? When does the church take time to stop, look, and listen? When does the church listen to God for its vision, purpose, and goals? When does the church ask, "Lord, what do you want us to do for world missions in 1998?"

I know what occupies most of the time church leaders spend discussing church business—and it's not, "How many missionaries can we send in 1998?" Church leaders carry the responsibility for setting the church's missionary agenda. Unfortunately, too often they see world missions as one component of the church program competing for time, interest, prayer, and money. In many cases, sending missionaries comes in dead last. Would it be asking too much for church leaders to spend at least one day a year together in a retreat setting, with nothing on the agenda but listening to God for his will for their church in world missions?

When the first missionaries—Paul and Barnabas—went to the harvest, they did not show up out of the blue as volunteers looking for support. They did not go to their church and say, "God has called us to be missionaries. Please help us." Instead, while the church at Antioch prayed and fasted (Stop, Look, and Listen), the Holy Spirit spoke and told the church to send Barnabas and Paul. It's time for our church leaders to follow the Antioch example. Of course, the model is not limited to the leaders. The church as a body must be called to pray and to wait upon God for his will. The missions program must not be a mandate handed down from the top, but a vision enthusiastically embraced by the members who are also looking for people to support.

The problems of church programs and budgets will disappear when the church decides to stop, look, and listen. What is God saying? Can we hear him? Or are our spiritual ears clogged with so many voices competing for the church's interest and money that missionaries are automatically dismissed?

Swarms of kids on the way

Hundreds of Canada geese settled on the pond be-hind our office, covering it like a cloud of mos-quitoes. My wife consulted her bird diary and discovered that her first robin sighting on March 10 was pretty much in line with their arrival in previous years. Also arriving on schedule are the teams of kids preparing to descend on the unsuspecting mission fields.

But not totally unsuspecting missionaries, of course. Many of them welcome the arrival of the youths every summer, eagerly anticipating their enthusiasm and seemingly boundless energy. They use them for everything from babysitting to teaching English to fixing up rundown churches and other mission buildings.

However, like an approaching thunderhead on the horizon in steamy June, we hear rumblings about whether or not it's really worth it to have thousands of American high school and college students hit the mission field for two weeks to two months each summer. I am not going to wade into this controversy and decide whether it's worth it or not. We have to be cautious, lest we dump a colossal wet blanket on the amazing spirit of our youth to do something good for Jesus around the world. Too often, I'm afraid, the missions theorists look at things so coldly that they fail to sit where the young people sit.

However, at the risk of appearing like a column of ants attacking your family picnic, I'm going to venture a few observations. First, not every junior high, senior high, or college youth who wants to taste life overseas for a couple of weeks ought to go. No matter how good they may be at painting, playing soccer, or plunking a guitar, not all of them are qualified and can justify the time, money, and effort needed to send them.

Second, some of our summer workers do more harm than good. They can be a drain on their missionary hosts. Sometimes they leave a bad taste in the mouths of the local Christians, the missionaries, and the regular folks around town. Some grumble and complain and never stop talking about how much better the U.S. is.

Third, they cost us a lot of money that could be better used in other ways. Just because the money is available from sympathetic people at home doesn't mean they ought to go. I'm thinking especially of those kids who try to raise $2,000 or $3,000 for two weeks of work in some far-off territory. There ought to be some correlation between their time and work on the field and what it costs to get them there. Many of them could get valid cross-cultural experiences closer to home and at far less expense.

We don't want to slam on the brakes, but for the sake of the young people themselves, their parents, their churches, and the missionaries on the field at least we ought to slow down for the flashing yellow.

To those tough enough and serious enough, who really want to explore something of what it means to be a cross-cultural witness, I say go for it for all you're worth. But it's no joy ride and if any mission tries to recruit youth on the basis of having a fun trip, the agency ought to repent. Even a short missions trip overseas is far different than finding your place in the sun and the fun.

So, as the season for summer missionary workers arrives, let's welcome it, not with flashier inducements, but with some serious head knocking and heart searching. The missionaries and Christians in Africa, Asia, Europe, and Latin America will be grateful.

The high cost of adoption

Before drug dealers began to litter our streets, and drive-by killers terrorized the neighborhoods, the bad guys were litterbugs. The cartoon litterbug was so ugly that we felt like stomping anybody who dared to throw a cigarette butt on the sidewalk. Confronted by far worse enemies, however, society has pretty much forgotten its war on litter. At least it has taken on a benign face. Schools, churches, and social clubs now adopt a mile of highway, promising to keep it litter free.

Adopting a mile of highway is not very complicated. We know what a mile is; we know whose mile it is to keep clean; we know how many people it takes to pick up the stuff; and we know if the right-of-way is indeed free of paper, bottles, beer cans, and assorted refuse.

A number of years ago, it occurred to some folks that the unevangelized people of the world could be parceled out much like a stretch of highway. Once they were identified by name, they could then be adopted (not assigned, of course) for purposes of evangelization by various mission agencies and churches. This plan became a movement with a name, Adopt-A-People Movement.

However simple the concept appears, cleaning up the world's vast millions of unevangelized people obviously is a far more difficult task than keeping a highway litter free. The people themselves often are not so easily identified. You can, of course, count them by color, language, religion, and nationality, but the boundaries around unevangelized segments are more fluid than fixed. They don't stay put like a mile of highway. One of the prime complicating factors is the unparalleled exodus from the villages to the cities.

Because the whole adoption approach is voluntary, and no one is in charge, we don't know whose job it is to evangelize a specific segment. Not only that, we keep getting in each other's way, because agencies, churches, and missionaries try to claim a particular "mile" as theirs, or at least they like to say they are the first and only agency working with that group of people.

But after we've adopted some people, then what? Do we really grasp the enormity and complexity of evangelizing them? Do we know how many linguists, evangelists, church planters, agriculturists, social workers, and so on, will be required? Do we know how many years of pain and suffering it will take just to establish a viable beachhead, let alone a survivable church? But we go ahead and adopt them anyway, so we can check off another "mile" as being reached.

We know when a mile of roadway has been cleaned, but how do we know when our adopted people have been reached? Take one of the largest and most prominent of these groups, Indonesia's Sundanese (31 million or so), for example. Numerous missionaries, churches, and agencies have adopted them, and some have already abandoned them, because adopting a people really gets tough when they resist our efforts to evangelize them. One missionary couple wrote to us: "In the past four years, we have seen 21 of our American co-workers leave the ministry to the Sundanese for a variety of (usually very good) reasons. This year alone, 12 people have moved on to other ministries."

Adopting was the easy part for these missionaries, their agency, and their churches. But now they've gone to other fields and the Sundanese remain unevangelized.

Perhaps neither the missionaries nor their agencies nor their churches knew beforehand what it takes to establish churches among them. Unfortunately, the mission field is littered with examples of miscarried adoptions. World evangelization cannot be done as easily as adopting a mile of highway.

The system still works

Our next-door neighbors Jim and Alice left today to be missionaries in Japan. More than geographical neighbors, they have been heart neighbors. We have studied the Bible with them, worshiped with them, and prayed with them, especially about their decision to quit their careers in publishing and teaching. We agonized and prayed hard over the last two years while they raised their support. Jim and Alice are typical of a new breed of "second career" missionaries.

Tough as it is to see them go, we celebrate their going because Jim and Alice prove the system still works. Our independent evangelical system for getting people into missionary service is ponderous and filled with potholes. It has been roundly criticized as outdated. A new book based on findings from focus groups across the country says there is "uniform discontent with the present deputation (support-raising) system."

Maybe so. Jim and Alice were frustrated and aggravated by the system, but they did not quit. They kept on working and praying, calling and writing, speaking, teaching, giving their testimonies, and telling their story to countless local church missions committees. Their faith was tested, and their faith grew. Their spirituality deepened. They never doubted that one day God would get them to Japan.

Why does this system that nobody likes still work? Because calling and sending people to missionary service is God's work. He starts it and he sees it through, because trumpeting the good news means more to him than it does to us and our agencies and our churches. This is God's business. He sent his Son and he is not going to allow our peanut-sized faith and inefficient bureaucracies to stifle his work.

If efficiency were the name of the game, I would have quit the missions business 50 years ago. If slick, easy methods were available to get people overseas into the devil's lair, we would get all the glory and God none. Friends, it's uphill against the devil every step of the way, so let's quit griping about how inefficient and tough the system is and start fighting with faith, perseverance, prayers, and sacrificial gifts.

The second reason why the system works is that God's churches and his people believe the gospel and they believe in making it known to people everywhere. People somehow manage to get into missionary service despite some hard-hearted, tight-fisted churches. Jim and Alice are rejoicing that not all churches and not all Christians turned a deaf ear to their needs. They knew that God had his people and churches out there somewhere to get them to Japan, and he did.

The third reason the system works is that there are still people out there like Alice and Jim who will persevere in obedience and faith. They are convinced that God wants them to do something to spread the gospel, so they will not be deterred. Just as Peter stepped out of the boat to meet Jesus, so Alice and Jim "stepped out of the boat" when they resigned from their positions, not knowing for sure if and when their full missionary support would come in. As long as we have obedient Christians who live by faith, and work hard, the system will work.

So we celebrate God's call and his goodness. We pray that many others will follow in their train. We pray that God's voice will not be stifled by fears about security and children's's education. We pray also that the system will be lubricated by generous, visionary churches and individuals, so that others like Jim and Alice will get on their way in short order.

The winning formula

The three wise men of Monday Night Football—Al, Frank, and Dan—are never at a loss to tell us why certain plays worked and others backfired.** They act like historians explaining why Washington won and Cornwallis lost. But digging through the scholarly tomes you realize there are certain common keys to victory on the battlefield, just like there are on the football field.

These keys go back to the Greeks and Romans, but they still work. For example, a reporter asked a military strategist how Rwanda's minority Tutsi rebels could possibly have driven out the far superior—in numbers and weapons—Hutus. He gave the classic answer: leadership, discipline, and commitment to a cause. The success or failure of the world missions enterprise also depends on whether we observe or ignore these principles.

Of course, we don't have to look to football coaches or generals for clues about how to win. But it is strange how often we look for and promote some secret play, some new research, some clever invention that promises to crash enemy lines. Each generation produces a fresh crop of discoveries designed to do for missions what fan jets did for airline travel. It's so much easier to be enamored with our quickness and our so-called breakthroughs than it is to immerse ourselves in building leadership, discipline, and commitment. Seventy-five yard touchdown passes—"the bomb" in football parlance—pull fans out of their seats more quickly than four yards and a cloud of dust. Mission boards that sell the equivalent of "the bomb" attract more candidates and donors.

But the person who designed the church's game plan did not talk about flanking maneuvers, feints, and trick plays. Jesus Christ is our leader, commander, and signal caller. His outmanned, outgunned players learned one painful lesson—their success depended on being shaped in his image. He was shaped by the cross, by total conformity to his Father's will.

The key to victory? (Jesus called it bearing fruit.) Live consistently in him. If we don't, our productivity will be zero, nothing, zilch. Scintillating strategies will evaporate into nothingness unless our leaders absorb and follow Christ's crucifixion model. Frankly, we pay far too little attention to the qualities of our leaders. Often, they spell the difference between victory and defeat.

Of course, the best leaders must have disciplined, committed troops. However, these classic qualities of first-rate missionaries seem to have been obliterated by more catchy, upbeat recruiting slogans. Mission agencies can score touchdowns, so to speak, only with missionaries who have developed discipline and commitment to a cause long before they filled out their application papers. In military affairs, disciplined troops follow orders and stick to their assignments. Their retreats are severely controlled.

However, our culture's values make it extremely difficult for Christians generally to control themselves. They find it hard to accept restrictions on their lives for the sake of world evangelization. Obeying God's will to enlist in some part of the missionary enterprise appears to be like volunteering for a root canal.

Once engaged in spiritual warfare in another culture, disciplined, committed missionaries will make a significant difference. They will stand and fight. They will follow their leaders in battle. They will prevail.

Mission agencies never outgrow the need for people like this. Rather than looking for more missionaries, they should look for better ones. Instead of chasing pots of gold and playing strategic lotteries, mission leaders— and the churches that grow missionaries—need to learn again the enduring values of leadership, discipline, and commitment to a cause.

When missions is a snore

The school bus pulled into the parking lot at **Northside Park where a cross-country meet was under way.** The driver had disgorged his load of loud kids and seemed relieved to be alone and quiet for awhile. Minutes later a young fellow stumbled off the bus with his backpack and mumbled something about having fallen asleep. "Can you imagine," the driver said to me, "how anyone can sleep in a bus full of screaming kids?"

"No," I said, recalling some times in my youth when

I had slept past bus stops. Now I sleep through scream-ing TV commercials. Actually, lots of people sleep through storms, fire sirens, and even revolutions. Entire congregations of people sleep through significant changes in world missions.

To be precise, these churches don't sleep, they just keep on doing the same old things. When it comes to advancing the gospel in strategic, creative ways, they might as well be asleep. They haven't kept up to date, so missions to the majority of folks is a huge snore.

Of course, many forward-thinking churches have adopted new ways of thinking about and supporting missionary work. Praise God for the tremendous support they give to new missionary strategies. Unfortunately, relatively few churches do this.

Waking up sleeping churches isn't easy. Like the man dozing in his La-Z-Boy recliner while the TV news an-chor drones on about earthquakes, civil wars, and politi-cal crises, churches have trouble sorting through the mountain of missionary appeals. Competition, ineffi-ciency, lack of planning, and high costs bamboozle the person who tries to make some sense out of missions. Every missionary talker sounds the same. They talk about places and people the Sunday morning crowd cannot connect with. They even speak an unfamiliar code language. "Wake me up when it's over," the man says as he nods off.

However, these folks readily acknowledged that their church ought to support some missionaries. Not to do so would be like denying the faith. So they plod on with a dull, uninformed approach to world missions.

Where is the alarm clock? Or, better, Who is the alarm clock? Excitement, information, and change come either from church leaders, or from a hardy band of thinkers and doers in the pews. In some cases, lay folks lead the charge over their sleeping leaders. However, it works, we have to raise the congregation out of its ho-hum attitude toward missions and missionaries.

Some brave souls have dispatched their pastors overseas, hoping and praying they will come back with vision and determination to change. Missionaries have offered to be adjunct staff members while on home assignment, maintaining high visibility in their church work and getting to know more people in informal settings. Missions committees and pastors have attended special conferences sponsored by ACMC and other groups.

Of course, despite the incredible competition they often face for the church's time and interest, missionaries can wake up people, too. They must be informed, credible, interesting, and available. They must paint a coherent, understandable picture. Why should people pray for and spend their money on them? They must serve their churches with prayerful confidence, knowing that God will wake up someone in that sleeping congregation, because he is the God who calls and sends.

The Home Front

A relic from the past

Remember the good old missionary conference? You started with a rousing missionary speaker Sunday morning and eight days later you finished with an appeal to young people to answer God's call to be missionaries. You know what? It worked. Hundreds of people first met missionaries, heard their first missionary stories, gaped at their first pickled snakes, and went to the mission field.

This is true. I kid you not. What I've described has never been witnessed by thousands of contemporary Christians in hundreds of evangelical churches. The eight-day missionary conference is a relic from the past. Relatively few people come out to hear missionaries any more. Christian young people pack out rock concerts, but not church missionary conferences.

I spoke at a church recently that has had eight-day conferences for 44 years, but the pressure was on to change the format. Should they change, or should they cling to a relic? That's like asking how long IBM should have held onto its computer mainframe business, while the world was chasing PCs.

Perhaps the most critical question, not just for church missions committees but also for mission agencies, is how to find a way to bring new missionary interest, vision, support, and prayer into the life of the church among the younger people. Of course, we should discuss mission conference formats, but the issue is not simply eight-day conferences vs. weekend conferences. No format is sacred. The one is not more spiritual than the other. Any schedule can become traditional.

Our culture has had a profound effect on the way we

use our discretionary time and money. For most people, going to church Monday night to hear a missionary is about as exciting as hulling a bushel of lima beans. When our culture changes family lifestyles, do we keep on bucking culture, or do we find other ways to connect our missionaries with people who need to get to know them and hear their stories?

Thanks to global television and jet travel, our missionaries are no longer the exotic creatures they once were. Why go hear someone just back from Liberia when you've just seen the civil war on TV? We've seen so much African wildlife on National Geographic specials that we don't gape at pickled snakes any more.

Conferences as special events on the church calendar serve to focus the church's attention on Christ's Great Commission. Its obedience can be measured in prayer, in recruiting, in giving, and in sending. Many churches use the annual missions conference to spark their faith-promise financial commitment to missions for the whole year.

Whatever their benefits—and they are considerable—relying on a conference to do the job is like relying on a Hail Mary pass to win a football game. Football teams that build spirit throughout the season, and learn how to knock down people who get in their way, will score touchdowns without last-minute desperation passes.

Somehow, 52 weeks a year, the local church has to infuse world missions commitment into every level of its program. That includes Sunday school, junior church, youth programs, and the pulpit ministry as well as the women's missionary prayer circles.

Relics make nice memories, but churches have to do more than pay fond respects to the past, because the world desperately needs to hear about Jesus Christ. Churches must never allow missionaries to be nice old relics. The world's culture, at home and abroad, must be successfully engaged so that we keep on sending people around the globe to win people to Christ. Whatever it takes, churches must work extremely hard to keep God's call to missionary commitment above the typical Christian's commitment to watching "Sixty Minutes" on Sunday nights.

Donor report cards?

The 747's wheels crunch into the runway with a jarring thud. Their nine-hour flight completed, Joe and Sally and their kids scramble to gather all their stuff tumbling out of their overhead bins. Forbidding questions pummel their minds as they stagger through customs and immigration. What will it be like? Will we fit? Will we look okay? Will we like the food? Will we pass inspection?

But wait a minute. This 747 hasn't landed at Manila, but at Chicago's O'Hare airport. These missionaries are not arriving on the mission field, they're coming home for furlough. Why are they so worried about coming home?

They won't know the latest "in" things to do, the latest fads, the latest slang, the latest fast foods, the latest TV shows. It will take them some time to take affluence in stride and not rebel against it. At first, the superficiality and superfluity of the whole evangelical environment will stun them. They'll wonder why some of their friends and churches have either reduced or dropped their support when they see the kinds of houses, cars, clubs, and church buildings their friends use. But perhaps scariest of all will be their appointments, not with their dentists and doctors, but with the missions inspectors who will demand to know what return they have received from their investment in Joe and Sally over the last four years. They've heard about such accountability sessions, about missionary report cards, about churches and donors demanding more "bang for their bucks."

One night, in the middle of trying to explain what they've accomplished, and trying to get the same, if not a little more, support for their next term, Joe and Sally turn the table on the inspector generals. "Hey, two can play this accountability thing," they say. "We're happy to give you our report cards, but could you give us yours?"

Embarrassed silence descends like thick fog. A committee member mumbles something he later regrets. "Uh, why sure, of course, why not? What did you have in mind?"

"Well, for starters," Joe says, "how many hours have you spent praying for us? How much evangelistic bang did you get for your bucks? What I mean is, How many people have you brought to faith in Christ this past year? Divide that into your church's total budget and see how much it costs you per soul. And what's your total missions budget look like compared to the rest of your expenditures?"

Sally notices a red tide rising above the collective collars. We'll be lucky to get out alive, she thinks. But, we're in over our heads anyway, so here goes:

"I was wondering if we could see some videos of your all-night prayer meetings," she asks. "That would help all of us missionaries to know you really do re-member us. That's tough, I know, so maybe you could tell us how many birthday cards you sent to your mis-sionaries. Or how many 'care' packages. Come to think of it, I don't think we even get your church newsletter. We'd sure like to pray for you, too."

Before the examiners can recover, Joe says, "Could we see the church's mission statement, your goals for next year, and your five-year plan?" Slam dunk. The game's over. It's a rout.

The missions committee learned that accountability is a two-way street. That's all Joe and Sally were trying to say. Missionaries don't mind turning in their report cards, but they would be greatly relieved and encour-aged to see their supporters undergoing the same kind of examination about their commitments to world evan-gelization.

Donor report cards, for individuals and churches alike, can include some of the simple things we often take for granted, but perhaps overlook in our zeal to be sure that our missionaries perform well. What a heart-warming thing for Joe and Sally if their accountability sessions began with their donors' report cards.

Mutual accountability is not like a Ping-Pong game. It's deadly serious business, because all of us in world missions one day will face the final exam when we stand before our judge, Jesus Christ. What will he in-clude on this exam?

Missionary report cards?

Parliament in Britain has stirred up a ruckus by proposing a radical idea: Schools should publish their examination results. "It is a brave MP who argues that parents should be denied information that could help them find the best school for little Johnny," commented *The Economist* (London).

A similar bombshell smote me the other day when a pastor asked me if I knew how his church could evaluate the work its missionaries are doing. To paraphrase *The Economist*, should churches and donors be denied information that could help them decide whether to maintain missionary support?

Who launched this rocket zooming over the missions horizon? Laymen who have returned from overseas work projects, that's who. They saw missionaries, and some they deemed efficient and productive, some not. They were not looking for numbers, but for good work habits, the kind they expect to see in their own businesses.

Some missionaries bristle like cats backed into a corner at the notion of laymen, or pastors for that matter, poking around. They reason that these visitors can't act like informed efficiency experts because they know little, if anything, about cross-cultural work.

I think missionaries need to realize a new day has dawned at home. It's a day when you can't depend on your missionary call and your board's acceptance of your qualifications as sufficient reasons for a church or donor to keep on supporting you year after year. People expect some kind of accountability, some record of deeds done, some idea of your work plan, some estimation of how well you are doing according to your plan.

Part of the valid reason for expecting a missionary report card springs from the spiraling costs of keeping missionaries on the field, plus the fierce competition among missionaries for support. To put it simply, churches and donors want to support the most effective and productive people because their funds are limited.

Another home concern is the apparent lack of close field supervision. Supporters know that in some circumstances missionaries are very much on their own, with limited supervision, and in some cases the temptation to underperform is very strong. In addition, some home offices often come up empty when churches ask, How well are Joe and Sally really doing? The churches suspect that no one knows.

Are they wrong to ask for a missionary report card? Not really. Why should anyone be insulted if people who pray and give sacrificially ask for at least an annual report card? (I mean something more than a prayer letter.) It should state some specific annual goals. This will stimulate intelligent prayer. At the end of the year it should tally hits and misses, with brief explanations. People love the big picture.

Beyond that, every field supervisor should prepare an annual evaluation of workers, so that church mission committee files are accurate and up to date. This will be a major part of determining support budgets. In too many cases, "the field" suppresses "bad news," as it were, so the church at home never knows when problems develop.

Good missionaries, like good students, have nothing to fear from report cards. The rest? For the sake of the churches and donors, at home and on the field, they should come home.

Thankless missionaries

Like smoke rising from a pile of burning leaves, nostalgia climbs into the air at Thanksgiving. Family, kids, turkey, football—it's a wonderful revival of our best traditions. We choke and kids giggle as we go around the table and say what we're especially thankful for this year.

A fellow told me how thankful he was after a critical hospital stay. He wondered how to give some reason for his hope to those who had cared for him. He thanked his nurses, and they told him not many people did that. He even called his insurance company and thanked them for paying his bills. They were overwhelmed. People don't do that, they just call to complain, argue, and criticize.

Why is it so hard to say thank you? Within a couple of months, two friends asked me that question. One was so upset that she vowed to stop sending gifts to missionaries who never said thank you. The other one did not go that far, but I could tell he was deeply troubled.

Ingratitude is indefensible. I do not accuse the entire missionary force, but when long-time givers are hurt by the sin of ingratitude, we must confess that even one ungrateful missionary is too many.

Part of it may be administrative foul-ups. I've received thank-you's from missionaries I don't know for gifts I never sent. I really can't say that every board scrupulously informs their missionaries about gifts received. I don't know how often they issue donor reports.

And perhaps missionaries don't pay attention to those reports. I know donors who annually give their missionaries a 5 or 10 percent increase, but most of them do not acknowledge their increases. I know people who give big money at special times, or for special needs, and their gifts are never acknowledged.

Reading through Paul's missionary letters in the New Testament, I'm overwhelmed by the number of times he said thank you. I confess my confusion when I compare his record with that of some missionaries. Do they take their partners for granted? Do they presume on their sacrifices? Do they assume their gifts will keep coming even without some acknowledgment? Or is it just plain laziness and lack of personal organizational skills?

People don't send money to missionaries to get letters telling them how wonderful they are. But if donors and missionaries see the missionary enterprise as a partnership, as Paul did, they will serve each other with courtesy and graciousness.

We teach our children to say thank you when they learn to talk. We require them to write thank-you notes to their relatives. But somewhere down the line we seem to have lost not only a social grace, but a biblical mandate.

Paul said thank you for people, not just their money. A thank-you note from a missionary really says I appreciate you. You are a friend and you stand with me in my spiritual warfare. Paul said Christ gave him all he needed through the people at Philippi who remembered him.

Is the sin of ingratitude for people rooted in ingratitude to God? Just as we cannot separate our professed love for Jesus from doing what he says, so we cannot divorce our gratitude to God from writing thank-you notes.

Saying thank you is not an option for missionaries. However they do it—by mail, phone, fax, or e-mail—

they must do it. When they are home, they must say thank you in person.

There's more at stake here than social formalities. What we need is the same depth of intimacy between missionaries and their friends at home as we claim between the Lord Jesus and ourselves. If some missionaries are either too busy or too cold to say thank you, I wonder what they are saying to people they are trying to win to Christ.

The day the missionary cried

The missionaries came back from their first term. The people in their home church eagerly awaited their report on Sunday night. The young man had been born and raised in the church, had committed his life to Christ in the church, and had received God's call to overseas service in the church. The bonds of love were very strong. Theirs was a textbook case of how God's missionary program is supposed to work.

He spoke first and briefly described what he had done. While not an exciting story, it nevertheless gratified the people, because one of their own sons had done his job well. Then his wife spoke.

· Rather, she tried to speak, but almost immediately she broke down and wept. A solemn hush fell over the congregation. Brave, successful missionaries are not supposed to cry in public when they come home.

But when she regained her composure, and blurted out the hardships of trying to raise her baby far away from her normal family support network, the people understood—at least the mothers did—and they wept with her. She did not belabor the point, and it was obvious she was not performing to arouse sympathy. Rather, she had decided to be candid, even if her report did not match the expectations of what missionaries are supposed to say in public when they come home.

By making herself vulnerable she stimulated the kind of caring support many missionaries only dream about. Her family was embraced with empathy and understanding that has stayed with them for more than two decades.

Unfortunately, it's very hard for most missionaries to appear anything less than invulnerable. Somehow, they think their reports had better glow with success. The entire missionary enterprise has become as strongly market-driven as the industries that sell us cars and toothpaste. Shiny cars and shiny teeth sell; so do shiny missionaries. If they expose any dents or chipped teeth, they may lose a measure of their support for the next term. Therefore, they have to keep on selling themselves to their constituencies.

Frankly, I'm more impressed by missionaries who cry than by those who assume we cannot stand stories of pain and suffering. You see, people at home are not fools. They know that missionaries face hardships. So they raise an eyebrow when missionaries act as if they're invulnerable. The marketing specialists' basic flaw is that they do not respect their audience. They think the money will not come in unless the audience is sold a bill of goods, a lot of gab and glitz.

Not only is this marketing approach sub-biblical, in terms of integrity and honesty, it undercuts the missionaries who admit they are human. They bleed and hurt, and they have colicky babies who make life miserable. They also face a less than hospitable environment—not just their living conditions but the powers of darkness that surround them.

Therefore, if missionaries are to gain the strong support they need to sustain themselves on the field, they must be candid with the folks at home. If this flies in the face of marketing theories, fine. I believe in the end both the sending churches and their missionaries will be much stronger, more courageous, and more persevering on the field.

So, missionaries, please go ahead and cry. Trust me. You will grow 10 feet tall in the eyes of your supporting friends. Your tears will be forever stored in their hearts.

The shoe polish test

Nippy **Jones died a couple of weeks ago.** He wasn't a retired missionary, Bible teacher, or professor of world missions. Nippy was a baseball player who didn't come close to equaling the exploits of either Babe Ruth or Cy Young. Nippy wouldn't be famous for anything, except for an incident during the fourth game of the 1957 World Series.

He was struck on the foot by an errant pitch. Ordinarily, that would have entitled him to first base, but the umpire said No, the ball never hit him. Nippy allowed that it had, so he asked for the baseball. He showed it to the umpire and pointed to the black spot on the ball. Shoe polish, Nippy claimed. That was enough proof, and the ump sent him to first. Later on, Nippy scored and his Milwaukee Braves went on to win the game and ultimately the world championship.

Every church should have some "shoe polish" on it

proving it belongs in the big leagues of world missions. Would there be any evidence that this church takes world missions seriously? Could you say, without a doubt, "There it is! That proves this is a missionary church?"

In our culture, we'd probably look first at the budget. We might look at the church's total giving to world missions, or to a percentage of church income that is expended for missions. Certainly the missions budget is one sign.

Second, we'd probably look at the number of missionaries and agencies on the support rolls. We could find the total, but that might not tell the whole story, because some churches give more money to fewer missionaries. We could look at the number of "home grown" missionaries.

Third, we could count how many people have been on short-term missions projects and trips. Or how many have taken a vacation to visit a missionary family. These are also helpful diagnostic tools.

There are other signs of "shoe polish" as well. How many people have a regular missionary prayer list? How many write, fax, or e-mail missionaries regularly? How many send special "care" packages overseas, and remember birthdays and anniversaries? How many have entertained missionaries in their homes? How many dig behind the news headlines and pray for missionaries according to what's happening in their countries?

We also have to look for "shoe polish" on the church's staff. Are the pastors knowledgeable and enthusiastic about world missions? Do they give missionaries ample time on the platform? Do they pastor their missionaries? Do they read missions books and periodicals? Do they pray publicly as well as privately for missionaries and world concerns? Do they pray for and encourage people to face God's call to both short-term and career missions?

Do they plan and promote special times of missions emphasis on the church calendar? Do they integrate missions vision into the Christian education and youth programs? Do they direct people in how to give more to world missions, so that the missions budget increases each year? Do they spend some time overseas? Do they expect accountability from both missionaries and their agencies?

Finding irrefutable proof of missionary commitment in a church is not as easy as finding shoe polish on a baseball. However, the signs must be there, or we are just kidding ourselves. Once a year every church needs to compare its deeds with its profession, even though such an examination is a lot more painful than getting hit on the foot by a fastball. We need to examine priorities and goals annually in the light of God's great missionary heart, vision, and commitment.

If we don't get in the game, and follow the rules, we'll never get to first base. The great umpire in heaven has been known to say, "You're out! I don't know who you are."

What's the church for?

Back in 1937 a huge snowstorm hit Salem, Oregon, **and caved in the roof of the tiny Christian and Missionary Alliance church.** Without funds for repairs, and with no hope for growth, the elders decided to close up shop. They told the 25 or so people to find other churches.

"You can't do that," protested one woman. "You can't close down this church," she insisted.

"Why not?" they demanded.

"Because our missionaries won't have a church to come home to," she explained.

Her logic compelled the brothers to change their minds. They found money to fix the roof, and today that church has some 2,000 people worshiping on Sunday mornings and supports 32 missionaries.

By refusing to allow her church to die because the missionaries needed it, that woman embodied the spirit of A.B. Simpson, the father of the Alliance. He knew the church exists for missions, to send people anywhere and everywhere to declare the gospel. He didn't invent that idea, of course. It originated with Jesus Christ and was carried out by the church at Antioch in Syria. But as we look at all churches past and present, relatively few have copied either Antioch or the Salem Alliance Church. We simply do not have our priorities straight.

Why not? Because churches see world missions as an adjunct, something like the men's bowling league or mom's club—the hobby of a special interest group. For years, churches have salved their consciences with the ladies' missionary society. This is not a put-down, because without these women, the torch of world evangelization would have flamed out.

But what about the typical churchgoer? How many can say their church exists for missions? How many can own Christ's mission to save the world as their mission? How many can see beyond the confines of their own lives, their own families, their own jobs, their own communities?

Researchers claim it's bad news to talk about "missions." Conjures up too many bad images, they say. You have to invent some new rubric, some new slogan, to attract people who have been turned off by mission boards, missionaries, and calls to missionary service.

Far be it from me to decry creativity. I'm for anything that will grab people and stir them out of their slumber and disobedience. But let's be candid. We have absolutely no assurance that new words will awaken the dead. Whatever you call it, unless church leaders and their people believe the church exists for mission, nothing much will change.

The critical mass must be moved by energy from on high—energy from pastors, councils, boards, elders, deacons. Unless they get the picture, nothing much will change. They will still delegate Christ's mission to a committee or a missions pastor.

When people walk into a church they must smell worldwide outreach for Jesus Christ as if incense were burning. The smoke of missionary passion must permeate the whole place, beginning with worship, pastoral prayer, and on down through all of the educational programs and various age and social groups. Everyone must boldly declare, "Our church exists for missions to the ends of the earth."

Pontiac loves to brag, "We build excitement!" We must do that in our churches. We need an infusion of excitement, like that which blew A.B. Simpson out of comfortable Thirteenth Street Presbyterian Church in New York City and into evangelism and world missions. He started the Christian and Missionary Alliance in 1887 as an informal fellowship of believers from various churches for prayer, encouragement, and world evangelization.

The woman in Salem had it right. The church lives for missions.

When the pieces don't fit

T WA's Flight 800 from New York to Paris lifted off one of Kennedy Airport's runways and headed east off the coast of Long Island. Shortly thereafter the 747 exploded and crashed into the Atlantic. Divers and salvage crews scoured the ocean floor for bodies and wreckage. Families of the victims, as well as the FBI, struggle to make the pieces fit, but they won't.

The families need the pieces to fit because huge, gaping wounds tear at their hearts. The detectives need the pieces to fit because unsolved mysteries strain their professionalism, put people at risk, and allow bombers to roam free.

Everything about our cultural and psychological makeup demands that the pieces fit. That's why we are so proud of our educational, scientific, and technological progress. Each new advance helps us to make more pieces fit.

This spirit of the age permeates our world of missions as well. Missionaries dread having to e-mail home that some pieces don't fit. Managers and fund raisers at home strive to present the perfectly successful mission. The risks are too great if they admit that the wheels came off some magnificent missionary chariot.

But perfection is not the real world. Yes, every day aircraft make the New York-to-Paris run safely. Charles Lindbergh did it in a one-engine plane. But once in a great while something goes wrong in an old 747 and down she goes.

Most missions are successful. People hear about Jesus, believe in him, start fellowships, and grow in their faith. Missionaries build schools and clinics, teach at Bible schools and seminaries, translate the Scriptures, treat the sick, provide relief for the hungry, broadcast on radio and television, distribute literature, and start businesses, all for the sake of making known God's offer of salvation in Christ.

But crashes—ugly, nasty, bloody—intrude into the real world of missions as well. Not everyone believes the gospel. Some who say they do turn out to be pretenders. Not all believers grow into the fullness of Christ. Some fight over leadership and property. Some turn into defectors. Churches become worldly. Institutions wither and die. Missionaries fight local church leaders as well as other missionaries.

What shall we do when the pieces don't fit on the mission field? Drag the debris to the surface and lay it out for all to see—just as they're doing in Long Island with the wreckage of Flight 800? We should search our own rubble like bomb-sniffing German shepherds for the same reasons that the search goes on in the Atlantic off Long Island. Deeply wounded people need to bring closure to the events that caused their bleeding. And those who run our mission boards need to deal with the causes so they don't happen again.

The apostle Paul faced disaster among the churches in Galatia. They had repudiated the gospel of grace and returned to legalism. Even to a man as sharp as Paul, the pieces did not fit. He tried again and again to figure out what had happened. Finally, he threw up his hands in despair and cried, "I am at my wits' end about you."

Some missionary prayer letter or public relations piece that makes. He did not try to hide the disaster. Rather, he sternly confronted the Galatians. (No "make 'em feel good" prophet was he.) His letter makes me wince, because he cared so much about the truth of the gospel. When the pieces don't fit, we should admit it and drive our stakes deeper into the gospel of God's grace.

Will the real missionary stand up?

"I thought missionaries were holy people, but now I know they're just like us." As discoveries go, this one by a teenager after a summer visit will not rank with landing on the moon, but close to it. Why? What images of missionaries have we created that cause people to fall into shock when they meet the real thing?

Perhaps the false image is a carryover from stories about the exploits of early missionaries. You had to be somebody special to do what they did. Another fact is that missionaries are a highly respected minority in the church. If you volunteer to leave home, family, and friends, and if you risk living among strange people on foreign soil, you must be somebody special—at least holier than most of us. If appreciable numbers of ordinary people did that, it wouldn't be so special anymore.

I also suspect there's a carryover of the clergy-laity distinction in the minds of many kids. By creating two layers of Christians, the pros and the amateurs, the church implants the notion that the pros answer to higher calling and therefore must possess some elevated degree of holiness.

It's also vital to keep the holiness image sharp in the minds of people at home, lest their ardor for the missionary cause languish like stunted corn in a drought. If any unholiness seeps through, financial and prayer support quickly disappears. Therefore, our brochures brim with happy stories about happy missionaries bringing happiness all around.

Should we then keep kids—and adults, for that matter—sealed off from the real thing? If the idol has feet of clay, what then? Should we keep our missionary on the pedestal? Or did that teenager learn something that might help him?

Probably most missionaries want to be perceived as real people—special in the sense of their calling—but not set apart as better or holier than the rest of us. When talking to children and teenagers, their honesty, integrity, and genuineness will speak powerfully.

I once asked a class of Bible college students to write about the visiting missionary who impressed them the most, and why. I was astonished when they were virtually unanimous, both in their choice and their reason. He was honest with us, they said.

They didn't mean the rest of the missionary chapel speakers were dishonest. They only meant that this man's transparency and integrity overflowed from the pulpit and in personal conversations afterwards. He was himself; he did not try to impress anyone with heroics, nor did he appeal for sympathy because of the hardships he had suffered.

Often I sense the tension in missionary speakers, because they want to be honest. Yet they know they have to give a good report, to make a good impression, to be winners and not losers. Sometimes only their private conversations reveal some of their frustrations. "Let me be me," they seem to say to us. "I don't want to be on the holiness pedestal."

The more open we can be around teenagers today, the more likely they are to think positively about missionaries and about giving their lives to serve the Lord Jesus Christ. We can certainly learn about the dangers of pretense and hypocrisy from Jesus. He was always simple, clear, and direct. He never made it easy to be one of his followers. He never sought applause and approval. He never wavered from his mission. He went about his Father's business, no matter what.

The
Resources

1928's prices
don't cut it today

Ever yearn for the good old days? I did when I got
The Time Chronicle for Tuesday, Oct. 16, 1928 (the
date of my birth), and learned that the price of a loaf of
bread was 9 cents, a gallon of milk 57 cents, a pound of
butter 57 cents, a new Ford $525, a gallon of gas 12
cents, and a new home $7,782 (avg.).

Those prices come to mind when people complain to
me about the high cost of supporting their missionaries.
Somehow, our memories are as good as last year's campaign promises when it comes to recognizing that just as
the costs of our basic foods and cars are not what they
were 64 years ago, neither are the costs of world missions.

We accept rising mortgages, groceries, cars, and taxes
like drinking our morning coffee. Nor do we blink when
our new church building costs anywhere from $10-15
million. But let a missionary family tell us it will cost
$65,000 a year to support them and we lift off like a
NASA space shot.

What has not changed since 1928 is the Christian
public's perception that missionaries are supposed to
live below the poverty level overseas and sacrifice the
stuff U.S.-bound Christians take for granted. It's okay for
us to have all the blessings of the good life, we seem to
say, but missionaries must not count on them. Being
taken care of and being a missionary just don't mix.

However, what has changed is that missionaries are
catching up to all the fringe benefits American workers
have come to take for granted. So today companies expect to pay, and workers expect to receive, health insur-

ance and pensions. As our whole culture has shifted in its expectations, so has the missionary subculture.

You can argue all you want that missionaries must live by faith and forgo health insurance, educational nest eggs for their children, and retirement plans, but that isn't going to change the fact that this generation of missionaries expects those benefits to be included in their support packages. Does this make them less spiritual, less faith-driven? No less than the people in our churches.

Missionaries are products of their time. Our time includes inflation, benefits, and a world currency market no longer dominated by the U.S. dollar. Missionaries are not extraterrestrial. They don't behave like E.T.; they behave like you and me, with the same needs, wants, and expectations. They are us.

Churches and individual donors have to move from 1928 to 1992 and stop griping about what it costs to put a missionary family on the field. But don't I know there's a recession on? Of course I do. I have friends in my own church who have been out of work for months. But I know more who are doing quite well, not just surviving but prospering. What concerns me is the attitude that suggests that missionaries don't deserve what we take for granted, and if a crunch comes along, they are the first ones to be cut from our personal and church budgets.

Money, as Jesus said, will always strike like a laser beam at the true state of our hearts. If missionary support is the first to go, then our hearts are not engaged in world evangelization. Money isn't really the problem, personal commitment is. No church, mission board, or missionary would be short of funds if people who claim to be Christians gave just 5 percent of their money away, to say nothing of the tithe.

Give your missionaries a cost-of-living boost each year at budget time. American workers expect it, so we should be glad to give it to missionaries, too. Tragically, many missionaries are locked into the same $25 or $250 a month they received when they first went to the field. It never occurs to many donors that missionaries need raises each year just to stay even.

While we accept all the benefits that our economy has provided since the end of World War II, we certainly must agree that missionaries are entitled to them, too. The money for missionaries will be there, if all of us take a brutal look at our own spending habits.

Fund raising: the "scent" of Christly?

This is the story of two phone calls. First, from a national charity:

"Would you like to contribute to . . . again this year?"

"No, I don't think so."

"Thank you." Click.

Second, from an evangelical relief agency:

"There's a terrible crisis in Sudan and we're calling to see if you could give $100."

"Well, I'd like to think it over."

"The need is urgent and we have to know today if we can count on you. Could you give less than $100?"

"As I said, I'd like to consider this along with other things."

"We really do need to know how much we can send to Sudan. Could you give $25?"

"No, not today, but please send me the information so I can consider it." Click.

We understand the great need in Sudan. No problem there. But why should Christians be subjected to arm twisting, even for a legitimate cause? Perhaps the agency will get its money and say that the approach pays off. But at what cost?

The whole cause of world missions suffers a black eye when agencies resort to this. It's hard to maintain a solid reputation in the eyes of the world, not to mention the church, when we stoop to such manipulation.

Mission boards have a duty not only to abide by biblical principles of fund-raising, but also to teach them to Christians and elevate giving to the spiritual grace it really is. The agency that called us violated the clear injunctions of the apostle Paul, to wit:

1. The gift should be given willingly, not after the squeeze has been applied (2 Cor. 9:5).

2. People should give after they have had ample time to make up their minds—by prayerfully considering the need along with other needs, and their own resources and ministry goals—and not under compulsion (2 Cor. 9:7).

Why do we who pride ourselves on our fidelity to Scripture so often stumble when it comes to fund raising? One reason, obviously, is that unseemly pressure works. Another is that we can't seem to bring ourselves to trust God to give us the needed funds through ways that might be out of step with modern fund-raising techniques.

People of faith? Oh, yes, we say. But show me your faith by your works. Comparing the two phone calls, it appeared the secular charity was more charitable toward its donors than the Christian relief agency was.

We are supposed to spread the knowledge of Christ throughout the world like a lovely perfume. Christians are supposed to have the unmistakable "scent" of Christ. (See 2 Cor. 2:14, 15, translated by J.B. Phillips.)

But when we back people against the wall and try to browbeat them into giving, we're stinking up the name of Christ. We're like a dog bounding into a dinner party after enjoying a roll in the yard.

If the leaders who initiate, or at least condone, this kind of unbiblical fund raising do not put a stop to it, the people should—by standing firm on their duty not to be pressured and to take every need before God in prayer.

Who knows? The agencies might be cleansed, God might send them a ton of money, Christ's name might smell good again, and unbelievers might come to repentance and faith.

Impetuous, impulsive giving

Disasters bring out the best in people, but sometimes that is not always an unmixed blessing. Take the case of Jarrell, Tex., devastated by a killer tornado last May. Shortly after, Jarrell was inundated with more donated food than it could handle, including 23,280 jars of spaghetti sauce, 63,360 boxes of spaghetti, 23,040 heads of lettuce, and 1,800 bottles of salad dressing.

Said one emergency relief official: "It's incredibly well-meaning. We just don't want to create a disaster within a disaster."

How often have our well-meaning relief efforts

around the world created disasters within disasters? To ask this question is not to demean the heroic efforts of relief workers, or the motives of America's donors, many of them compassionate Christians whose hearts are touched by the suffering caused by earthquakes, famines, and plagues.

One the other hand, if we do not ask it, we risk creating more disasters within disasters. For example, many relief experts, as well as students of foreign aid politics, believe that part of the blame for the agony in former Zaire (now called Congo) could be laid at the feet of well-meaning humanitarian efforts on behalf of the Hutu refugees from Rwanda.

However, as Christians we do have some serious responsibilities to consider before—metaphorically speaking—we ship 23,040 heads of lettuce to Jarrell. Too often in the past, it seems to me, we have done the equivalent. Why? Because Christians respond impetuously and impulsively to a crisis or disaster.

Perhaps such response is better than giving nothing at all, but we do not have to choose between impulsive giving and no giving. It's far better to give prudently than impulsively. We have to look not only at the immediate needs for food, blankets, and medicine, but also at the longer-term outcomes. For example, when a local village is inundated with tons of grain (usually far more than can be consumed or stored), what does this excess grain do to the local market price of grain? In many cases, it drives farmers out of business.

Admittedly, Christians in America may not be privy to all the facts on the ground in some remote corner of the world, but they should at least make the effort to become better informed. The last thing they want to do is create an unbreakable cycle of dependency. We must examine the books, so to speak, and look at the track records of those who use our money for disaster relief.

We also must examine some relevant biblical records. The first missionary church at Antioch not only sent Paul and Barnabas to evangelize and plant churches, it also sent relief to Jerusalem. But the saints did not give impetuously. They had ample time to study what to do. My guess is that the believers studied, prayed, and waited on the Holy Spirit in regard to this matter just as they did before sending their first missionaries. That's the pattern we must follow.

Likewise, the apostle Paul warned against impulsive giving. He told the Corinthian Christians that their giving should be thoughtful, planned, systematic, and sacrificial. For Paul, giving was the exercise of a grace gift, not an emotional reaction to a television commercial or a letter in the mail. If we do our homework and study the needs and the long-term outcomes, as well as the Bible, God will save us from sending 23,040 heads of lettuce to people who don't need it.

One soul for a million $

Quick! **What do you remember about Benjamin Harrison, 23rd president of the United States?** Was he a Republican or a Democrat? Did he serve one term or two? Well, this one-term Republican (1889-93) is probably best remembered for having defeated Grover Cleveland, despite winning fewer popular votes. He also signed the Sherman Antitrust Act. Did you remember that?

But here's a curious fact. For some reason (I wish I

knew) he went to the big ecumenical missionary conference in New York in 1900. (That was before "ecumenical" became a bad word in our circles.) There he met a most unusual woman from India, Lilavati Singh, a graduate of the first women's college in India started by missionary Isabella Thoburn. By the way, she overcame the prevailing view of her male colleagues, succinctly stated by that great pioneer missionary to India, Alexander Duff: "You might as well try to scale a wall 50 feet high as to educate the women of India."

Anyway, Isabella Thoburn brought Miss Singh to speak to American Christians. Her brilliance and eloquence amazed them. They said her addresses were "beyond the depth of the average preacher." So impressed was President Harrison that he said, "If I had given a million dollars to foreign missions, I should count it wisely invested if it had led only to the conversion of that one woman."

"A million dollars for one soul? No way!" say today's keepers of the ledgers in the offices of foundations and church budget committees, as well as individual donors. No, nearly a century after President Harrison's accounting system, we are virtually enslaved to the "more bang for the buck" evaluation of our missionary work. Mission agencies and missionaries have to prove themselves to the chancellors of the exchequers by showing how many conversions they have produced for the money invested in them.

Of course, no one knows what an acceptable return is, but I guarantee no one would find one soul for a million dollars acceptable. What about 50 conversions per million, or a thousand? Jesus said you cannot put a price tag on anyone's soul. He said the value of one soul is so incalculable that the angels sing when only one person is converted. Should we say, "Waste of time!" to the angels?

Yet as we follow Christ's program for world evangelization, we have to raise more and more money. Missionaries have a hard time with people who say they can't afford to support missionaries, because they cost too much. In other words, one soul isn't worth it.

For example, a typical couple with no children has to raise better than $5,000 a month to work in Japan. "Is one Japanese soul worth that much? Where does all that money go? That's an enormous salary for a *missionary*!"

My italics show that missionaries are never supposed to make as much as people who stay home. Be that as it may, people should know by now that "support" includes a lot more than salary, because the churches now demand all kinds of member care, leadership, and training—plus health insurance and a pension. Missionary support is like the sticker price of a new car. Mission boards struggle with how many "options" to add to keep the same people happy who complain about the high cost of missionaries.

We all stand before Christ's accounting system. We don't own anything, because he owns us. We will have to account for every farthing, whether we keep it for our selves or give it to someone who can bring another Lilavati Singh into his family.

We have to look at world evangelization in the light of Christ's judgment of our total investment in his cause. The question is not, How many conversions per thousand dollars?, but, What kind of investments are we making under Christ's ownership of our time, money, and opportunities?

Saving lives, not dollars

Illinois, where I live and work, is one of three states **that do not require motorcyclists to wear helmets.** Every two years our legislators take up such a law, but routinely vote it down. Their simple logic seems to be that if people want to kill themselves, fine, let them do it.

During this year's debate one of our local radio stations interviewed a spokesman for the "right not to wear a helmet lobby." The reporter sharply probed the issue. As you might expect, they differed on the potential harm to the state's economy and budget through diminished motorcyle sales. They differed on the higher costs of hospital bills, insurance bills, and taxes. They differed on the potential loss of federal payouts to Illinois.

Suddenly, I felt like yelling, "Hey, you guys! Why don't you argue about crushed brains, destroyed lives and families, lifetime disabilities, and death itself? Are these irrelevant? Can't you debate the value of a human life? Why are dollars the only issue?"

Like a boomerang, my challenge to the debaters came winging back and smashed me in the face. In our passionate debates about missionary work, what are we liable to argue the most about—dollars or lost lives? Let's honestly admit how often dollars dominate our discussions. Dollars dominate our plans. Dollars dictate our strategies. Dollars decide who goes to the field and who doesn't, what gets done and what doesn't, what gets built and what doesn't, who stays on the payroll and who doesn't.

Dollars corrupt our relations with churches overseas. Dollars eat up our people. Dollars consume the brains and energies of our most talented leaders. Dollars shape our prayer letters and our furloughs. Dollars decide who's in charge and who takes orders.

Meanwhile, all over the world people's lives are snuffed out like so many motorcyclists ramming into trailers, trucks, and trees. These are the people who supposedly God has called us to save. What are they worth? Where do they figure in our plans?

Our task, it seems to me, must be to shift our missiological field glasses away from dollars and toward human beings. They must occupy center stage on our agendas. When we think, plan, and pray, we must think, plan, and pray people, not budgets.

The world's people must be resuscitated from sterile numbers and become living, breathing, dying human beings just like ourselves. Our statistical charts show "hidden," or unreached peoples. We are urged to adopt a people. These people march across our literature like so many little ducks in the old-time shooting galleries in the penny arcades. We even identify them as targets.

Our new missionaries are well indoctrinated in this bloodless agenda. We risk making missions a sanitary, soulless science, devoid of life-saving transfusions. In our rush "to get the job done" we scamper around the globe like circus advance men handing out tracts, claiming to have evangelized someone.

Mission, in the biblical sense, means suffering and bleeding for our fellow sufferers and bleeders. It means hours, days, weeks, and years of loving someone, whether this person takes our tracts or not.

Our next consultation should not be on the crisis of missionary support, but on the tragic shortfall in listening, loving, and serving skills. How do we discover someone's hurts, fears, and deeply held traditions? We ought not send anyone as a missionary who has not earned some credibility with some unbelievers somewhere. Our experts should be those who have clothed themselves in the feelings and convictions of other people.

We must not permit money to upstage human lives on our missions agendas. The question is not what it costs to require helmets, but how many lives it saves.

The parade of Rolls-Royces

People will do almost any crazy thing to set a world record. In a comic strip, two kids are peering over the side of a bridge into a pond and one of them says, "I doubt if there's a world record for spitting on bugs." Perhaps not, but the idea isn't too far-fetched, if you look at some true stories.

One that intrigued me last summer happened in Beverly Hills, California, a likely setting for the bizarre. The new record was set by owners of Rolls-Royces, who formed a cavalcade of 125 cars, the longest unbroken procession of Rolls-Royces ever assembled. The previous record of 114 was set in 1991 in Hong Kong.

A mile and a half of Rolls-Royces glittering in the California sun projects a powerful image, not just of wealth but of the state of the world. Pretend that the owners of the 125 Rolls-Royces had paraded their swanky cars not through Beverly Hills but the streets of south-central Los Angeles, which are still lined with gutted-out storefronts, the remains of the 1992 riots. No, we can't even pretend. Such a painfully preposterous juxtaposition of wealth and poverty is just too damning.

But that's the way the world is, people riding into the sunset in magnificent automobiles while millions of others have barely enough to eat and drink.

As Christians, we suffer ambivalent feelings about this wicked disparity. It's not (I hope) that we covet being in the parade of Rolls-Royce's, but that we feel a shade uncomfortable about Christ's judgment of how we spend what we think is our money. Don't we suffer a slight twinge of conscience when we move into bigger houses? The larger issue, of course, is why God gave us all this money. What does he expect in return? Why has he decided that the American church should be so rich? And, most worrisome of all, will the roles one day be reversed? Will we trade our luxury for agony and torment, as happened to the wealthy man and Lazarus the beggar?

To be serious about world missions means we can't treat questions like these as if they were pesky flies spoiling our picnics. Too often, it seems, we grab our flyswatters and flail at what we think are our problems, when the real problem may be in the garbage can.

For example, mission boards need money for their candidates and projects, so they appeal to Christians and churches for more. Often it's like squeezing blood from a turnip. What we lack in our churches is not money, however, but some compelling reasons to give it away. Indeed, we must give it away, not just to balance the inequities between what we have and what the world needs, but to save our souls. Our surfeit of money will kill us.

No, the world will never equalize ghetto-dwellers and Rolls-Royce owners. Their simultaneous parades of ostentatious wealth and grinding poverty will go on until Jesus comes. But if the word and example of Jesus Christ mean anything to us who profess to believe in him, then we have to tell each other quite bluntly, "Give your money away." For the sakes of those poor in spirit and in body, and for our own sakes. To save their souls and ours. That's why the funding of world missions is so much more profoundly spiritual than squeezing blood from turnips.

If you think parading Rolls-Royces through burned-out Los Angeles streets defies imagination, try this demonstration: Jesus Christ, though he was rich, became poor for our sakes, so that through his poverty we might become rich. Try to figure out the mathematics of that trade-off, and then ask if you are willing to become poor so that someone else might become rich.

Tired of appeals? Give more

If there's one criticism of world missions that seems to be heard more than any other, it's that the sponsoring agencies are wearing out their welcome with persistent appeals for money. These appeals come through the mail, over the radio and television, and in person. The agencies, for their part, respond that the world is far from evangelized, more people and projects are needed to meet the existing needs and opportunities, and their costs are going up just like everybody else's.

Doubtless, some appeals are irrational and play fast and loose with the facts on the field. Some promise quick cures and spectacular results for the donor's investment. Some agencies, contrary to Scripture, appeal to impulsive giving, playing on people's emotions and guilt. Some suggest that you will get more "bang for your buck" by supporting them than by giving to someone else. Competitiveness creeps in like an ugly slug in your tomato patch. Truth, integrity, humility, modesty, and fairness should be the hallmarks of every appeal for money.

On the other hand, when some people cry about fund-raising excesses, they need to be reminded that, generally speaking, precious little of our money goes to world missions. Now, that doesn't excuse the violations of good taste and honesty that unfortunately do occur, but it does put the needs of mission agencies in a somewhat different light.

For example, according to the latest U.S. figures available (1988), religious and welfare activities accounted for 2.4 percent of our personal expenditure. That came to $76.1 billion, compared to $246.8 billion we spent for recreation. However, of that $76.1 billion for religion and welfare in general, only $1.7 billion went for overseas work of U.S. foreign mission agencies. On a global scale, researcher David Barrett (*World Christian Encyclopedia*) estimates that Christians give .017 percent of their income to world missions.

Perhaps those numbers are little comfort to the besieged donor, but on the other hand, it seems clear that many Christians go on responding to advertisers' appeals and they never complain; rather, they spend, spend, spend for lots of products and services they really don't need. Why, then, should they complain about the mission agencies' persistent appeals for their money, when that money can be used to reap eternal rewards for themselves and for millions of people who need to hear the gospel, be trained in the faith, and be helped out of poverty, illness, illiteracy, ignorance, and exploitation?

No, we have no right to complain about appeals for our money for missions. Those agencies are doing us a favor, provided we respond with our grace gifts systematically, sacrificially, and intelligently, and not out of either pity, or guilt, or malice.

It would help, of course, if those who need our money would also teach us how to give it. Because giving is a spiritual gift, we need to be taught to "excel in this gracious work also," according to the apostle Paul (2 Cor. 8:7). Until they do, however, we are without excuse for a very simple reason: We have lots of money and the mission agencies need lots of it. May this year be a year not only when givers give more, but also when nickel-and-dimers and those who give nothing would discover the joy and satisfaction of digging deeply for world missions.

What's happened to service?

Once upon a time, I banked at a friendly small-town bank. Years passed and the little bank grew and prospered. One day a much larger big-city bank swallowed up my friendly small-town bank, and I became a cipher. I grew tired of signing in and waiting for a so-called "personal" banker, so I went to another bank.

The people there know me and look after me. I don't have to sign in as if I'm a patient waiting to see the doctor. Instead, I've been offered coffee and a newspaper. One day I waited a few minutes to sign some papers.

Nadine left her desk, brought them over to me, explained what it was all about, handed me a pen, and I signed them right there in the easy chair.

There's a simple word for this—service—and it's almost as forgotten among our mission boards as it is by huge commercial banks. Our mission boards could not exist without their depositors. They take in our checks and pass on our deposits to their workers and ministries. But how do they serve their depositors?

Of course, the law requires the boards to send us a receipt. We also get a duplicated thank-you note and another envelope. They send us magazines, newsletters, and special appeals. They invite us to their banquets to get more checks. Unfortunately, such "service" often is a cloak for recruiting and fund raising.

Sadly, it seems, some boards sense no duty to serve their depositors in other ways. Not part of their mission, they say. They think everything should be directed to getting more of their money, not nurturing their depositors. Fund raising and marketing consultants tell them to drop their magazines because they don't bring in money. Boards tell their candidates how to raise money, but not how to serve those who support them.

Such attitudes and policies are misguided, shortsighted, and unbiblical. God's servants are responsible to serve those who make their ministries possible: Pray for them, teach them, build them up in their faith, increase their knowledge of God's will and of the churches overseas. Mission board leaders need to read the apostle Paul's letters to his depositors with service in mind.

Service should include offering churches unfettered help in growing their missions passion and knowledge. Instead of looking at everything through the lens of income, boards must give away their expertise, knowledge, and zeal for world evangelization by every possible means. Their service must exude enthusiasm for the whole of world missions, not just their narrow, parochial interests. They have to interpret for us what God is doing in the church and the world, not just what they are doing.

How can mission boards better serve their depositors? Minister to our needs. Feed us God's word. Aim at our hearts and minds. Save us from our greed, our comforts, our love of money, our passion for self-fulfillment. Forget recruits and money. Deliver Spirit-empowered truth. Don't preach and print hype and hokum. Don't preach to us until you've first bathed yourself in prayer and the word of God. If your people don't have a fresh touch from God, don't send them to our churches.

Send us Christians from the churches our mission boards have started overseas. Our boards should spend some of our deposits to serve us through the eyes, hearts, and souls of the people we have invested our money in—Asians, Africans, Latin Americans, Europeans. Soak us with their tears and their visions. Drench us with their passion for Jesus. Scour us, burn us, rebuke us, if you must, but lift our eyes to the world's harvest fields as Jesus did.

We're not ciphers on your computers. Serve us best by saving us from ourselves. We need you. "Sirs, we would see Jesus."

The Cultural Challenge

"Fedexing" the truth

Federal Express Corp. taught America how to deliver packages overnight. Perhaps the ultimate tribute to the company's success is that "Fedex" is a verb meaning to ship small parcels. But in places such as London, Paris, and Berlin you don't "Fedex" it, you "DHL" it. (DHL is Federal's chief competitor.)

Even though Federal Express has poured $1.5 billion into expansion abroad since 1985, it lost $200 million over the last nine months. What's the problem here? To quote one critic: "Federal Express is one of the finest examples that the rest of the world is not the United States of America." For their part, Federal Express people say they're not that naive and eventually they'll get out of the red.

Future corporate balance sheets will tell who's right, but in the world missions business, our productivity and success overseas are not subject to bottom line accounting. Our "stockholders" (the people who pray and give) receive regular reports, both from the home office and from workers on the field, but those reports do not have rigid categories such as "earnings per share."

If they did, missions stockholders would begin to ask tough questions, such as "You have poured $5 million into Kenya. What do you have to show for it?" It's relatively easy to arrive at the mission's investment figure, if you know how many missionaries are there, what it costs to support them, and what it costs to maintain the institutions and support bases, like schools, hospitals, printing presses, radio stations, bookstores, and so on.

But quicker than you can yank your finger off a hot pot, defenders will rise up and protest that you can't quantify spiritual work that way. Of course, God's gracious Spirit works in ways nobody will ever be able to count, but that's not the point. We all want to learn whether our missionary investments are reaching our self-proclaimed goals. Federal Express wants to make money overseas, not lose $200 million over nine months. If the company is losing, people inside and outside it have a great responsibility to find out why.

Same thing in the world missions business. It's never wrong to ask why. I suspect one reason for our losses (or lack of growth) in some places is that a number of our boards have failed to grasp that "the rest of the world is not the United States of America." Occasionally, mission boards succumb to pressures to export the latest American innovations in evangelism, Christian education, radio, literature, music, youth work, and so on. In the schools where future missionaries study, the success models often are American.

Not only do our exports not always work, but the missionaries who take them overseas can fall into the "American-made is better" attitude. The church overseas, despite its years of spiritual maturity and practice, is looked upon as minor league, needing a good dose of American professionalism.

In the end, what do we really have to export? The truth about Jesus, but not wrapped in American packages, and not delivered by American methods. We ought to deliver the truth the way Jesus did: with humility, love, sacrifice, caring, and respect for people's integrity—with everything he had in mind when he said, "As the Father has sent me, so send I you." If we do that, he promised that "our fruit" would remain.

Feeling the game in your heart

World Cup soccer brings out the best (and some would say the worst) in nationalistic aspirations. Missionaries found themselves glued to TV sets. They cheered and agonized with the fans of their adopted countries. France won and missionaries there were amazed when the normally blasé French celebrated like Americans whose team just won the Super Bowl. Brazil lost and at least one missionary kid I know of plunged into despair.

Sportswriters in the United States generally mocked the poor showing of the U.S. team, but one of them, Bob Foltman of the *Chicago Tribune*, said he wasn't surprised. His explanation was simple: "How many soccer games do you see American children playing? Just a group of children in the park playing soccer with no coaches? Hardly any. And it's on those playgrounds or in the parks, just playing, not being told every step of the way how to do things, that skills are developed, creativity formed, imagination fostered."

Coaches can teach kids the basics of the game. They can tell them where to pass from certain positions. They yell at them to find the open man. In other words, the kids learn to play by the book, the safe, acceptable patterns.

However, kids can learn the game themselves by trial and error. They can learn how to improvise. If Plan A fails, they'll switch to Plan B. They learn these things on the streets and playgrounds, the way U.S. basketball players hone their skills. Special players develop in their free time, not in mechanical devotion to packaged drills.

Learning evangelistic missionary work is a lot like learning how to play soccer. Learning how to be a skilled, creative, imaginative evangelistic missionary begins with free play. On the streets, in the schools, in offices, on production lines, in parks.

Our schools and churches have developed a host of valuable evangelism programs. But at some point we have to learn to go it alone. Our schools and churches are the normal training ground for most missionaries. In our zeal to train, have we overlooked the values of free time, experimentation, and improvisation?

As I read missions history, I'm struck by the great improvisers who, in effect, threw away the books and developed something indigenous, something their own, something that fit their circumstances. In our day Bruce Olson is perhaps the best example of this, although there are many others.

Sometimes the people who learn to be evangelistic missionaries on the streets and in the parks do not always fit the patterns we have established for acceptance by mission agencies. We would much rather stick with those who have come up through the ranks and have done what the books and coaches say. Admittedly, it's hard to know when a person who has learned the game on the streets is really qualified for our teams. But I think our scouts probably miss a lot of great talent by not watching what's happening outside our normal coaching and recruiting channels.

One of Chicago's pro soccer players is from Greece. When asked the difference between American soccer players and those from the rest of the world, he pointed to his heart. They feel the game in their hearts. They weren't taught the feeling. It developed by having a ball at their feet and playing, playing, playing, every day in the parks, in the streets, going out and finding the game and their own creativity.

That's the way it should be for those who would be superior evangelistic missionaries.

More than hot air

The race to be the first to take a hot-air balloon around the world reminds me of those intrepid sea captains of yesteryear who sought to circumnavigate the globe. More than a few washed up on distant shores. The latest balloonists went down in Myanmar (Burma).

However, those 15th- and 16th-century voyagers were not trailed by television cameramen. No one sent pictures of their failures back home to Spain, England, and Portugal. But we were privileged to watch the gigantic balloon being chased by crowds of excited Burmese as it came to rest in their backyards. While it floated gently overhead, some of them shouted that it was the Buddha. The resemblance was not hard to see.

Balloon or Buddha? Hot air or the real thing? We may chuckle at the naiveté of the Burmese farmers, but how do we know that the Jesus we take around the world is the real Jesus? When we tell our stories to people who have never read or heard about Jesus, what perceptions of him fill their minds? How can we be sure that our gospel is not just a lot of hot air? How can we know that when people encounter Jesus for themselves in the Gospels, our version will not come crashing to earth?

Philip Yancey confesses in his book *The Jesus I Never Knew* that the Jesus he knew in Sunday school as a child—and later on as a student in Bible school—bore little resemblance to the Jesus he found in his study of the four Gospels. One has to wonder how much of the Jesus we have taken to other people is simply a replica of the Jesus of Sunday school and Bible school.

More than one missionary has been surprised when accosted by a convert who asks why the missionary's message and the message of the church is not as radical as that of Jesus. We have to ask if the countercultural teachings of Jesus have gripped our own hearts, souls, and minds. If not, then we do not have to look too deeply for the reasons for discipleship failures among our converts.

Many of our missionary-founded churches are struggling to maintain a distinctive witness. Their spiritual cholesterol levels are dangerously high. Their early enthusiasm for Jesus has disappeared into the quicksands of materialism, power struggles, greed, and tribalism. Did these converts ever meet the whole Jesus of the Bible, or were they simply introduced to the flannelgraph version of Jesus holding a lamb in his arms?

If our gospel is to be more than hot air, we have to tell the whole story of Jesus. For example, on my bookshelf directly above my computer I look at titles like these: *The Hard Sayings of Jesus* (an older and a more recent one), *The Example of Jesus*, *Jesus: Lord and Savior*, *The Teaching of Jesus*, and *The Parables of Jesus*. Any one of these books, plus Philip Yancey's, will take us far beyond the ABCs.

Until our discipleship training takes our converts beyond the flannelgraph Jesus, they will be like so many tons of herring swallowed by whales, consumed without ever having come to grips with all that Jesus taught and demanded. They need more than simple outlines and lists. Perhaps we find some of his ideas too hard to take. If so, we need to check our commitment to his lordship.

We desperately need a fresh infusion of evangelists and teachers who have met the real Jesus and perhaps stumbled a time or two trying to do what he says. We must allow our Asian, African, and Latin American sisters and brothers to bless us with their stories of the real Jesus. Perhaps too many American churches are floating on hot air, while the real Jesus takes root far beyond our shores.

Our American cake

The staff of a seminary in Africa threw a big graduation ceremony and party. Government ministers and foreign ambassadors came to the event. One of the American missionary wives baked a chocolate cake. An African who had been to the U.S. tasted her cake and said to her husband, "I tasted something American about it the very first mouthful."

Write that down as another new slant on cultural sensitivity. Apparently our missionaries even taste American. If our cakes have that unmistakable American taste, what about our gospel, our programs, our way of doing things? No matter how hard we may try, we cannot shed our Americanism like a snake sheds its skin.

However, we say that our gospel is transcultural. It's universally applicable. It fits any people, anywhere, any time. Jesus said people everywhere must hear his good news. He did not limit his mission to one people, language, religion, or culture.

Therefore, Christians continually fight to take America out of their cake. The fight rages not only in Africa but in the United States, where the gospel makes little sense because of the inroads of popular culture and biblical illiteracy. We cannot assume that anyone knows anything about simple Bible stories, let alone the reason why Jesus came, died, and rose again.

For example, I listened to a sermon that included repeated references to "the old man," without any explanatory comments. I began to think about the multitude of meanings "the old man" could possible have in that audience. We have to make sure our biblical and cultural terms really mean something in today's world.

Of course, we cannot remove basic Christian ideas from our language. We cannot risk stripping the gospel of its deep-seated theology about sin, salvation, and judgment. We face the difficult task of taking things that are hard to understand and making them understandable, whether in Africa or the U.S. But before we try to do it in Africa, we should have some success doing it in America.

We can never take America out of our cake, but in our presence and in our proclamation we must bend over backwards to avoid the smell of America. For one thing, America smells bad in many parts of the world because of the sensual, materialistic culture we have exported. It's even worse because this bad odor emanates from a country that is part of Christendom.

Therefore, as gospel messengers we live so that people can distinguish our lifestyles from what they see and read about. We are sorely tested to follow a different standard, one set by Jesus, not by our culture.

Jesus said that he lives in us so that people will get some idea of who he is and why he came. People want to see Jesus. They may not understand our theology at first, but if they see Jesus in us we will have ample opportunities to tell them why we love and serve him.

When I was a kid, growing up in Hershey, Pa., I loved to tour the chocolate factory and watch those giant granite rollers smashing through huge vats of milk chocolate. Back and forth, back and forth, they relentlessly made sure Hersheys was the smoothest chocolate on the market. The presence of tiny bits of granite never inhibited my consumption of Hershey bars.

For sure, some of America will always be in our gospel cakes. That's okay. People will eat them if they taste our integrity, love, understanding, acceptance, and patience. Our job is to see that the taste overrules any foreign elements in our cakes.

The Americans are coming!
The Americans are coming!

Back in 1966, when we weren't too far removed **from the Cuban missile crisis, some enterprising film producers decided to spoof America's paranoia over our Russian Cold War enemies by making a comedy hit, "The Russians are coming! The Russians are coming!"** Because of an emergency, a Russian sub crew actually landed in a tiny New England coastal hamlet, but common sense prevailed and no shots were fired. Fortunately, no one in the Pentagon ever found out about it.

Now, the shoe is on the other foot. For the sake of both U.S. mission agencies and Eastern Europe's Christians, we need a 1990s version, called "The Americans are coming! The Americans are coming!" Suddenly, after 40 years of clandestine missionary activity carried on under the noses of the communist governments, our agencies are gearing up for open spiritual warfare and the natives are scared.

Our intentions are good (just like the Russian sub crew), but can we be trusted to behave like good Christian ladies and gentlemen? In the film, the New England burghers weren't sure about the Russians and they found themselves looking down the barrel of a cannon. To carry the analogy a bit further, some Eastern European Christians fear they may be looking down the barrel of a huge U.S.-financed and U.S.-directed missionary cannon.

What they fear is that we won't do our homework, we won't take time to read our history books and we won't appreciate the strengths of the existing churches that have been there for centuries before we Americans ever had a single church on our soil. This, after all, is the era of American-dominated missionary effort and while the Eastern European Christians appreciate our concern and our generosity, they are wary of our tactics, our individualism, our buying out local people, and our penchant for public relations and fund-raising gimmicks and gold mines. To be blunt, they fear being used, subverted, and sidetracked by the American missionary avalanche.

Of course, it's painful for a local Christian who needs our skills, our training, our resources, and our money to be forthright about his fears. The truth is, Eastern Europe's churches and Christians are woefully short of all of these things. They desperately lack the bare essentials—enough Bibles and books—that we glibly take for granted, print too many of, and throw away. That gross imbalance of resources must be rectified.

These churches and people lack good Bible schools, solid theological training, seminars, workshops. Therefore, our mission agencies are trying to figure out how best to meet these critical needs. Our concern here is that our strategies not be unilateral, totally U.S.-based and U.S.-inspired. The situation is fraught with peril, because in the days of secret missionary work in Eastern Europe, more than 320 agencies were up to something.

All we ask is a measure of humility, of servanthood, of asking, "How can we help you do your thing?" rather than, "Here we are. Help us do our thing." Plus huge doses of partnership, with deep appreciation of and respect for the qualities, gifts, and spirituality of Eastern European believers. Unfortunately, our past record is not unblemished in some places where we blithely ignored the local people. Now, we have a chance to do better—a surprising open door to minister Christ to undernourished believers. Let's park our American missionary invasion models on the junk heap and work out a new model based on mutual respect and trust.

The lesson of the pea patch

Peter Piper picked a peck of pickled peppers. Remember that one? Earlier this summer Peter Piper (me) picked a peck of sugar peas. My own, actually. I had planted them late last March and there they stood, clinging to the wire with tantalizing beauty. I could taste these sweet little green gems even before my wife tossed them into the stir fry.

I reached through the wire and nipped off every sugar pea I could find. I was sure I had plucked them all. But then I backed up about six feet and saw lots more pods dangling among the leaves.

Then I backed off at an angle to my left. More peas. Then to my right. Sure enough—more peas. Finally, I crawled over the wire and stared at the vines from the opposite side of the row, and picked some more peas. That was Saturday night. Monday morning I went out to water the cauliflower, looked across the garden, and spied one more pea pod right out in the open. How could I have possibly missed it?

Isn't it frustrating when you are absolutely, positively, 100 percent sure you have seen all there is to see, and it turns out that you were looking at things from only one angle? How embarrassing and humbling to find more truth when you look at something from a different perspective. We need to learn the lesson of the pea patch: What you see head-on is not necessarily all there is.

How valuable it is to look at the "peas" from as many angles as possible before jumping adamantly to conclusions. If we don't, we'll miss at least half of the harvest.

When we take Jesus to people of different cultures and religions, let's step back and look at their lives from as many angles as we possibly can. Most of the time, our hasty conclusions only sever the jugular vein of communication. Rushing in to declare our beliefs, and to judge people and their beliefs, we fail to see why people believe and behave as they do.

Every person's values are a valuable composite of centuries of traditions. There's a rich lode of information to be mined, if we would take the time to back off, think, ponder, ask questions, and approach the issues from every conceivable angle. What we see the first time is only a sliver of the whole picture.

We have to apply the lesson of the pea patch to our relations with each other in the missions business here at home, too. I wonder how many times we have argued and split simply because we thought we had the whole truth. Our spiritual nearsightedness is appalling. We think we have all the peas in our basket, simply because we can't imagine that the other pea-picker would have any in his. We are simply blind to all the peas on the vine because we will not back off and consider the matter from the total perspective of 360 degrees. I probably could have found even more peas if I had climbed my step-ladder and looked at the row from above, or crawled on the ground for a worm's-eye view.

How refreshing it would be if we left our smugness at home. How spiritually invigorating if once in a while we simply confessed that what we see at first glance is not the whole story. When we gather to plan and pray for evangelizing the world, rather than target people "over there," perhaps we should first spend time confessing our spiritual myopia. If we don't admit that we see through a glass darkly, how will we find the harvest? That's what I learned picking peas.

The peril of drive-thru mission work

Speed drives everything today, from the computer business to fast-food restaurant chains. Everything, that is, except Amtrak. My recent train trip from Chicago to Lancaster, Pa., took almost 18 hours, compared to 14 when I first rode the Broadway Limited 40 years ago.

I'm not always so slow. Driving home from St. Paul, Minn., a couple of weeks ago we pulled into a McDonald's drive thru (that's the way they spell it), ordered some coffee and stuff, eased around the corner, and waited and waited. The drive thru's speed evaporated, our agitation climbed. Finally, we paid up, grabbed our sack, careened out of there, and got back onto the interstate.

That same demand for speed seems to have permeated world missions activity, creating drive-thru missionaries. According to the latest statistics, they far surpass the number of ordinary, we're-in-it-for-life, so let's-take-time to-soak-up-the culture-and-language missionaries.

Speed compels people to jet into a country for a week or two and then jet home again. Their speed is justified by both opportunities and convenience. Doors are open. We may never have a chance like this again, so let's get in as fast as we can. Besides, people are lost without Christ, and we have to hurry up and get there before they die.

It's easy. We can raise the money without too much difficulty, we don't have to take any courses in missions, we don't have to learn any foreign language, and someone will be there to take care of us.

Perhaps it's time for our missions executives to get off the jets and take a long train ride, so to speak, and ask, Why the rush? What trade-offs are we making for the sake of speed? At the very least, we need to evaluate the result and implications of our mad dash for more drive thru missionaries. The question is not, Are they doing any good? Of course they are. But immediate good results by themselves ought not foreclose our search for some long-term consequences.

The real question is, What kind of lasting results do we get from drive-thru mission work? This is really a biblical and theological question, because not all results are the same, as Jesus neatly pointed out in his parable of the sower. Drive-thru work may produce results that disappear like the fast-starting crops in the parable.

Have we been tricked into thinking there are speedy shortcuts into the kingdom? Do we ignore everything Jesus and the apostles taught about the high price of fruit and the critical importance of our fruit remaining? The whole point of the book of Hebrews is not how many started the faith race but how many finished it. All Israel was "saved" out of Egypt, but only Caleb and Joshua lived to tell about it.

How many bodies are we leaving to die in the wilderness because of speedy, drive-thru mission work? Isn't that the legacy of our drive-thru work in Japan immediately after World War II?

We have to retool, take stock, and pay attention to the Bible. We cannot allow the world's passion for speed to overwhelm our biblical and theological judgment. Our goal is not how many drive thru missionaries we can rush overseas. Our goal must be fruit that perseveres through adversity and remains faithful to Jesus Christ. To that end, let's slam on the brakes and look for the plodders who will stay with the fruit until it matures, no matter how long it takes.

One day Jesus Christ will judge our fruit. He won't ask how fast we got in and out of Russia. He will decide how much of our fruit will last and how much of it will go up in smoke. If we burn rubber in missions, all we'll get is smoke. That's the real peril of drive thru mission work.

The Obstacles

2000: The great diversion

Like huge thunderheads rising ominously in the western skies, the year 2000 approaches, arousing unbelieving fear in some segments of the Christian community. Christians respond to urgent appeals to stockpile food, guns, and ammunition. *Time* magazine noted these fears—and the actions spawned by them—and contrasted them to the Book of Revelation's call to prayer. The paranoia aroused by the coming of a new millennium amounts to a great diversion from what Christians are called to believe and do.

God does not call Christians to panic but to passion, not to self-preservation at all costs but to self-denial. If we are not careful, 2000 will sweep us into meaningless speculation and prevent us from devoting our energies to world missions and evangelism. If we put saving our own skins first, people who do not know Christ will face seriously diminished prospects for hearing and obeying the good news.

Already Christians are being ridiculed for some of the things they are saying and doing in view of the immi- nency of 2000. In some respects, they are simply follow- ing the footsteps of the utopians and millennialists who plagued America in the late 19th century. Their argu- ments remind me of the Cold War debates 50 years ago when we were told to build and stock bomb shelters in our backyards.

The church has always suffered from what I call bomb-shelter partisans, who seem to forget the mission Jesus gave us. Rather than retreat, run, and hide, Jesus told us to advance in the power of the Holy Spirit. God creates fearsome worries among the populace so that

Christians can stand boldly and courageously for Christ, offering hope and salvation, not bullets and death.

2000 ought to remind us not of places to hide but of places and people who have yet to come to worship Jesus as Lord and King. 2000 ought to force us to ask why the church has been so slow in taking the gospel to people and places where there are no churches. 2000 ought to bring us to repentance and renewal for deeds undone, and for disobedience to the Great Commission. 2000 ought to force us not to stockpile goods for ourselves but to invest all we have for Jesus.

The rising panic proves that even Christians have their minds set on earthly things, not on things above. 2000 ought to force us to confess that we are citizens of heaven, not of earth. 2000 ought to make us declare to a worried world that we look to heaven, not just as our escape hatch, but as a place from which our deliverer will come.

"Stand firm in the Lord" is what we should be telling each other. As we enter the countdown, and endure the hoopla and the false prophecies, we must call each other to exercise our hope and joy in the Lord Jesus Christ. He is our deliverer. We trust in him, not in our hoarded food and guns.

As we anticipate 2000, we should plan to gather in praise and thanksgiving. We should ask ourselves how we can do better than we have done in the past. Why has Jesus not returned for 2000 years? What expectations does he have for his people? Without a doubt, he wants to make us more like himself. Without a doubt, he wants us to enlist in his worldwide harvest, the building of his church, and the growth of his kingdom.

The antidote to fear was written a long time ago in

the words of a well-known hymn: "We rest on thee, and in thy name we go." Missionaries of the church have landed on distant shores with this hymn ringing in their ears. We can do no less as we stand on the threshold of a new millennium.

A foul wind blights our mission

S omething stinks across the country, and the odor is fouling the world like a blast of greasy air from **the back of your local hamburger stand.** No, it's not political corruption, or greed in corporate headquarters, or drugs and crime in the streets. It's moral defection and devaluation in some of our high profile churches.

It's revealed in current debates over whether or not to change the biblical rules covering sexual conduct. In various ways some church scholars and bureaucrats have actually succeeded in bringing their proposed changes to the deliberative bodies of their churches. Ultimately, according to this process, what is either acceptable or unacceptable sexual behavior is to be decided by someone's vote.

The argument boils down to this: Public standards have changed, and the churches ought to get up to speed. "Come on, people, let's jump in and join them!" seems to be the call. That's my interpretation of the logic that says any kind of sex is okay, so long as it is responsible, mutual, honest, and "full of joyful caring," to use the terms of one proposal.

So what? we evangelicals might say; this is just another example of liberals going down the drain. But wait a minute. Consider the missionary implications. Apart from sowing the seeds of their own destruction, the church people clamoring, "Down with the out-of-date biblical standards" are also blighting the church's world mission like a crop-duster spewing poison on thousands of acres of California lettuce. Only these folks are not killing insects; they are killing the church's witness to a world wallowing in sexual filth.

Imagine you are a missionary trying to interest someone in a "less-developed" country in improving his or her life. Among the many benefits you offer through the Christian faith is an improved moral standard, free from the curses of sexual abuse and immorality. And then this person stuffs a newspaper or magazine in your face and says, "What are you talking about? Don't you know your American churches are voting on whether fornication, adultery, and homosexual acts are okay? What are you American Christians up to, anyhow? How hypocritical of you to export that to our country."

Whatever any of the churches in America do thunders around the world and is slung into the faces of missionaries. Not only our standards of sexual conduct, but also the way we profligately spend our money on ourselves, and the way we routinely accept divorce as a way out of our marriages. Sure, missionaries have to take it on the chin from exported U.S. movies, television, books, and magazines, but from the churches, too? Sadly, all of this summer's church debates about sexual conduct have grabbed a big press. Regardless of how the votes come out, damage control will be difficult for missionaries.

This whole mess shows how, for a number of what seem to be logical reasons, it is perilously easy for churches to quickly fall into the trap of looking to their own interests first, and thus betray the Great Commission. We cannot blithely ignore the peripheral effects of our public deeds on millions of people worldwide, the people who are supposed to be the church's first concern. Whether we're voting on liberalizing moral standards, hiring more staff, or building multimillion dollar edifices, we send powerful signals around the world about where our priorities really rest.

Cancer or carnality? Which is worse?

My wife and I were enjoying lunch in the kitchen when the phone rang. I answered. It was the doctor saying he had just received the lab reports which showed that I had lymphoma. He recommended that I make an appointment with an oncologist right away. We choked and tried to get a grip on ourselves. There is no easy way to handle news like this.

Neither is there an easy way to handle the news we received from a missionary friend of long standing just a week or so later. In an entirely different—but no less devastating—way, our friend confessed to immorality, told us he had to leave the field with his wife and children, and that he was undergoing counseling.

Ordinarily we might think that cancer is worse than immorality; that chemotherapy is worse than counseling for chronic sin. I'm not so sure. One thing I am sure of: Normally we tend to pray more about our physical health than we do about our moral and spiritual health.

We tend to ask God to protect our missionaries from a host of ills, but we do not usually ask God to protect them from sins of the flesh.

When I received my friend's letter, the first thing I did was rebuke myself for not praying for his sexual purity. I've prayed for his support to come in, for his visas to be granted, for God to bless his work and use him mightily. But not to keep him pure.

The things I asked God to do for him were good things, right things, helpful things, but my prayers did not cover the full scope of his needs. I should have known this from the counsel the apostle Paul gave to his teammates. He did not shy from warning them about the perils of sex and money, for example.

One reason we do not pray for our missionaries' sexual purity is that we mistakenly assume they will not be tempted, and if they are, surely they will resist. After all, they are godly people called to serve the Lord. That's true, but they are still human beings, subject to the devil's attacks through every conceivable means. When we look at the record, we have to admit that more than a few missionaries have succumbed to sexual temptations.

I don't want to picture this as a moral epidemic, but I do want to raise our consciousness when it comes to praying for our missionaries. In our private times of prayer, we must ask God to make our missionaries morally strong and pure. We must ask him to give them the strength and courage to resist temptation when it hits them.

The typical missionary is no different from the rest of us. We know what battles we face in a sexually perverted society in North America. In some parts of the world, missionaries are subjected to even worse sexual provocations. Their hearts and minds must constantly be infused with the Holy Spirit. Sometimes, the very busyness and exhaustion of their ministries make them more prone to fall into sin. Their minds go wacky when they are away for long spells. They do things that ordinarily they would never even think about doing.

Our missionaries need power in ministry and in personal holiness. We all do. When we commit ourselves to pray faithfully for missionaries, we must enlarge the scope of our praying to include resistance to immorality of all kinds—not just sexual temptations, of course. This is a crucial part of our commitment to them and to Christ.

Thank God for the prayers of God's people for my physical, spiritual, and emotional needs. I wish for the same kind of prayer to cover all of the needs of our missionaries.

E-mail addiction

"In shock in Texas" wrote Ann Landers a tragic tale about her husband's on-line affair with another woman.** He had told his wife that it was simply a diversion and all in fun. In the end, however, he filed for divorce and decided to marry his on-line romance.

A missionary e-mailed headquarters that he was overwhelmed. Not by marital problems, but by e-mail. People e-mailed him just to find out if he received it "way over there in Africa."

I've heard e-mail touted from the pulpit as the way to get people in the pews "really involved with our missionaries." Now, the speaker said, you can read all the latest missionary e-mails posted on the bulletin board in the foyer. When I looked afterwards, no one was reading them.

Of course, for all of these horror stories, I could tell many about the benefits of e-mail. Nevertheless, it is time to raise the yellow caution flag, to slow down some of the speeders on the e-mail track who may be headed for serious crashes. And I don't mean computer crashes.

Society generally acts first and thinks last. Missionaries and churches usually do the same. As University of Chicago historian Pastora Cafferty says, "There is no question that technology drives culture. But during the time that the culture is being changed by technology, there is very little assessment of the positive or negative consequences of its use, especially unintended and unexpected consequences."

What are some of the unintended and unexpected consequences of e-mail on our missionaries and their work? I've heard again and again that e-mail consumes too much of their time. Computer addiction is no joke. It not only ruins marriages, it swallows whole the time missionaries should be spending with their families, their national coworkers, and people who need to hear about the Lord Jesus Christ.

E-mail also drives a deeper wedge between the technological haves (missionaries) and the have-nots (the local people). On-line capabilities draw missionaries closer to their families and home offices, but farther from the people they supposedly serve. As the *Financial Times* of London notes, "While the developed world experiments with exotic network applications, such as shopping and banking from home over the telephone, the majority of the world's population has yet to make a telephone call."

West African theologian Tite Tiénou says the world now has "fast" and "slow" countries. Fast is good; slow is bad. Admitting that most African countries are slow, he asks, "Why do we need to be fast when being slow works for us? More important, is fast really helpful in mission?"

We in the West are driven by our technology. We assume fast is better for ourselves and for the work we do overseas, even in slow countries. This makes it even more difficult to tell the good news in understandable ways.

My advice to new missionaries is to spend your first two or three years drinking coffee with the locals, learning their language, and finding out what burns in their hearts. Then when you've earned the trust of the people and the right to be heard, tell them the old, slow story about Jesus. Telling a story around a table at a sidewalk cafe is better than firing e-mail letters around the globe. The people whom God has placed in your care need your time and your love more than anything else.

To church missions committees, I say by all means use e-mail to keep in touch. But don't look to e-mail alone to revolutionize people's prayer lives, or to pump up their passion for your missionaries.

Food processor religion

Reflect on India for a moment. What pops into your mind? Calcutta's teeming slums? Millions of villagers barely hanging onto life? Religious radicals killing each other? Monstrous problems, to be sure, but perhaps none of them are as demoralizing as syncretism in the church.

"Syncretism"—now there's a word your average American Christian is about as likely to understand as nuclear fusion. Is it a rare tropical disease? A new political philosophy? As scary as AIDS? Because we don't know what it means, we aren't likely to pay much attention. If it's bad, something like deer ticks that spread Lyme disease, then we'll try to avoid it, stay out of the woods, or, if we do have to hike in infested territory, spray ourselves with repellent. ·

Syncretism is a religious disease. All of us do have to hike through dangerously infested territory, and there's no popular cure on the market. Look it up in the dictionary, and syncretism doesn't sound frightening at all: "the attempt or tendency to combine or reconcile differing beliefs." Rather harmless? Not on your life. Syncretism destroys the gospel and robs Jesus Christ of his claim to be the only way to God. If syncretism is good, world missions is a monstrous hoax and a dreadful waste of time, money, and lives.

Back to India, where the Evangelical Fellowship has taken to the rooftops, so to speak, and warned that syncretism will destroy the witness of the church. Here's the "smoking gun": Last January, the Synod meeting of the Church of South India blended Shiva, Buddha, Allah, and Jesus Christ. It was like taking Hinduism, Buddhism, Islam, and Christianity and throwing them into a food processor. Nothing really distinctive comes out; that's the genius of both a food processor and syncretism. You're left with a hopeless mishmash of "religious understanding."

The more palatable word for syncretism, at least in the U.S., is pluralism. Christians are supposed to be nice and tolerant, and stop insisting that theirs is the only true religion. Pluralism (and syncretism) says that all faiths have merit, they're all equally valid and "true," and so we should stop all of this evangelistic nonsense, especially among people of other religions.

People really do hold pluralism as a creed, disregarding the obvious (to me, anyway) fact that two totally different ways to God cannot both be true.

The more this idea takes hold in our churches, the less likely people are to be captivated by Christ's Great Commission. What's true in India is true in the U.S., and anywhere else, for that matter. If Christians do not confront syncretism, and expose its falsehood, the church's witness at home and abroad will be cut down like a silver birch tree after a couple of years of drought. One spring you look out the door and guess what? No new leaves sprouting on your birch tree.

World missions won't die overnight. The inroads of syncretism may be imperceptible at first. But eventually the roots of world missions will be denied the nourishment of God's word. Candidates and money will dry up. Why bother evangelizing Muslims, Buddhists, Hindus, and Jews, if they're all safe with their own religions anyway?

Never one to dodge a bullet, the apostle Paul boldly declared, "Christ Jesus came into the world to save sinners—of whom I am the worst." Had he wanted food processor religion, he was the perfect candidate: He could have blended what he called his own "faultless" religious observance with some new ideas from Jesus. Instead, he labeled his old Christless religious perfection "rubbish."

Pastors, theology and missions professors, and missionaries must join ranks with the Evangelical Fellowship of India and expose syncretism with both the incisiveness and compassion of the Lord Jesus himself. Otherwise, we might as well take the gospel and hang it up to dry in some museum of historic, but dead, religions.

Friendly fire

The Pentagon reports that human errors caused the "friendly fire" disaster in Iraq last April. You'll recall that 26 people died when our jets shot down two of our own helicopters. "Friendly fire" simply means you're killed by your own people, not the enemy.

Such incidents are not uncommon in the annals of warfare, but what about the front lines of missionary warfare? How much human error can we accept? How many casualties are tolerable from "friendly fire"?

Perhaps the very idea of being "shot" by one's fellow missionaries seems incomprehensible to the folks at home. I've never lost a son in battle, but I can well imagine how useless such a death would seem to be if it were caused by our own troops. In much the same way, the churches at home are not prepared for "friendly fire" casualties among their missionaries.

After all, we send our people to the mission field to engage in spiritual combat with people who are enslaved by the powers of darkness. Theirs is the ultimate battle, the battle for the souls of women and men. Such warfare is uncompromisingly severe, intense, and physically, emotionally, and spiritually draining. Theoretically, at least, we are prepared to accept some missionary casualties, especially if we read the Bible and church history.

But what a tragic waste when our casualties come not from the enemy but from our friends, our fellow missionaries. No, I'm not creating science fiction. The missionary toll from "friendly fire" is a well-kept secret, but it is not fictitious.

You have to dig out these stories as you would a tick from your leg. They don't come out easily. It's just as well they are not widely publicized. But that doesn't mean we have to pretend these missionary casualties from "friendly fire" do not exist.

Many theories have been propounded about why, in the words of Paul, missionaries "keep on biting and devouring each other." Of course, the simplest answer is that they are not perfect yet; they share the same flaws the rest of us do. So, one reason they do it is because all of us do it, to some extent at least.

But from there on the reasons get more complex. Some say Satan gets the jump on them and attacks them just because they are on the front lines attacking his strongholds. Others think it's because living in an alien culture often makes it tough to get along. Little things that people slough off at home grow like huge boils. Added irritants include such things as different home habits and standards, close proximity and lack of privacy, and lack of experience in a team setting. We just don't have much training and skill in working together. I once sat in a team meeting where they argued about when and where to have a picnic.

Criticism just seems to gush out of our pores. Missionaries squabble over doctrine, codes of conduct, strategic concepts, and, yes, "office politics," all the way from the team itself to the home office.

If I had to pick one explanation, I'd land on the

theory that the enemy's most successful tactic is getting us to fight each other. That way, we consume our energy on fratricide, rather than on winning the lost. Lest I be accused of picking on missionaries only, I have witnessed the same successful strategy in churches, Christian colleges, and other Christian ministries.

Why then air this "dirty laundry" about missionaries? For two reasons, at least. One, we have to prepare new missionaries to watch out for "friendly fire." Two, we have to alert people at home, so they can pray more specifically for their missionaries, that God will deliver them from infighting, from a critical spirit, from consuming themselves on themselves, and from finding conspiracies among their fellow workers.

George's resignation

In this parable, George's missionary career was on **the rise.** He had done well with language school. He loved and respected the people and their culture. The church had responded favorably to his teaching and training, so well, in fact, that it had invited him back for second and third terms. His sending board anticipated that he would become field director. His home church sensed that its hopes and goals for him were being reached. Suddenly, with the quickness and devastation of an earthquake, George resigned. Why?

All of the partners in the missionary enterprise— schools, churches, and agencies—struggle like ancient woolly mammoths in an Alaskan mud pit to find some answers. Probably nothing causes as much consternation in the missions community as losing effective missionaries. Were George's training and preparation some-how deficient? Did his church miss some signals of discontent? Was his sending board remiss in orientation and evaluation?

The liabilities on the world mission balance sheet are horrendous when people like George resign. He and his family suffer enormous grief, pain, guilt, and uncertainty. Like a rock in a pond, George's self-worth plummets to the bottom. His confused supporters raise all kinds of awkward questions: Moral problems? Family problems? Run-ins with the national church? Conflicts with missionaries?

The national church, of course, feels rejected. George's resignation, at least to some, proves that Americans just don't have what it takes. Church leaders, who believe one of their trusted allies has betrayed them, suffer because of the void in their ranks.

George's home church wants to think the best, but the missions committee wonders if the agency is to blame. Members worry about the impact on younger people who are praying about becoming missionaries themselves. Some of them think about the hundreds of thousands of dollars poured into George's ministry.

Back at mission headquarters, staff people shake their heads, dumbfounded. If George can't make it, who can? Some of them point to a trend in the mission—longevity of service continues to drop to around 14 or 15 years on average. They see this in other agencies as well. While some of the old, grizzled veterans mumble about the deficiencies of the new breed of missionaries, young staff rise to George's defense and say it's a complex problem. After all, about one-third of all corporate business managers on overseas assignments come home early, too, victims of what executives call "transitional burnout."

The corporate world has figured out that most of their early returnees do so because of personal and family stress. George faces the same things, but because he is a missionary he fights a kind of spiritual combat that can leave him on the streets for dead. George's insidious enemy attacks him in many guises. Sometimes it's outright persecution; other times, misunderstanding, doubt, personal conflict, worry. The apostle Paul lumped them together as the "care of the churches," and he did not have a wife and kids.

Paul said that servants of the gospel suffer and struggle. Some of his best fellow missionaries did not stay the course. At death's door, Paul warned Timothy about the hardships to come and pleaded with him to endure, to fight the good fight, to gain the winner's wreath.

I'm sorry George resigned, but I'm not mad at him, or his school, church, or agency. Sometimes, of course, flagrant oversights do bring the best missionaries down. But many times people like George resign because they have been pushed—or they push themselves—beyond their limits of endurance. Rather than blame them, we must nurture them back to health and self-esteem.

Gospel junk food

All natural. **No additives. No preservatives.** These labels on supermarket products promise us that we'll eat pure, unadulterated food. What about consumers of the gospel overseas? Are they getting the pure, unadulterated message? Or are they getting a gospel soaked with American additives? Are they getting the organically grown New Testament gospel, or a gospel sprayed with Western pesticides and fertilized with superficial American easy believism?

No question worries me more. My greatest worry is not about money or people for missions, or the strategies and management of missions. It's about the contents of the package we call the gospel—the cure for people's sins—and whether we have administered the real medicine.

I once attended a study conference where missions scholars and executives wrangled for a weekend, trying to define conversion. But I've never been to one where the gospel itself was addressed. We just assume we know. This can be a fatal assumption, especially for new missionaries. Missions seminars come in 31 flavors of ice cream, so to speak, but none of them discuss what constitutes pure ice cream. Some flavors are denominational, some are not, but that's not the main issue.

The consumer uprising took dead aim on junk food: It looks good, tastes great, but—depending on the product—it either lacks essential nutrients, or it's packed with stuff that does long-term damage. So it is with the canned gospel we stack the shelves of the world with. It can be loaded with unbiblical additives (various rules and traditions to keep). It can be seriously deficient in life-giving ingredients (no repentance, cheap grace, no biblical foundation).

The results of consuming either kind of canned gospel are disastrous. Some converts are constipated by legalism, perhaps living in constant fear of whether or not they will be accepted by God and judged fit for heaven. Some live in a fool's paradise, shallow in their commitment to Christ, or, much worse, devoid of eternal life because they have never met Christ's demands.

Therefore, it is imperative that we do what the apostle Paul demanded of the Corinthians: Test yourselves, examine yourselves, lest you fall under judgment. Our zeal for self-judgment has never matched our zeal for getting converts. We've been too busy counting people who raise their hands to ask if they really understood the gospel. Have our converts lasted? Where are the marks of legitimate conversion and discipleship? What kind of churches have we spawned? Do our overseas churches simply mimic American models, not just in worship styles but in the theology of the gospel they teach?

I see a Western missions establishment feverish about strategies (both at home and overseas), but woefully reticent to talk about theology. What is the gospel? is a theological question. But theology is now the abandoned child of world missions. Instead, we demand missionaries who are experts in as many skills as there are brands of baked beans.

We raise missionaries suckled at the breasts of television luminaries, some of whom do not major in strong theology, but rather in making coming to Christ as easy as entering the Publishers Clearinghouse Sweepstakes.

Our critical need is for people who have grappled with the purity of the gospel. They do not have to lay aside their denominational flavors, but they do have to be 100 percent certain that the gospel they teach and preach is neither deficient in essential doctrine, nor adulterated with American additives.

How we answer the question, What must I do to be saved? is the difference between heaven and hell.

Have I bugged you lately?

Our spring flowers erupted two weeks early. That's the good news. The bad news is that our winter was so mild that the bugs survived. There are bound to be some bugs in even our best church mission strategies. NASA expects every space shuttle launch to be bug-free, and that should be our expectation when we serve the Lord Jesus Christ in his great world evangelization plan.

Unfortunately, sometimes we launch things too quickly before we exterminate all the bugs. When something goes wrong, we're tempted to look for bugs in the wrong places, or for the wrong kids of bugs. We check our plans for flaws; we inventory our resources once more; we use the best research we can find. On paper, this thing should fly, but instead it crashes and we lose time, money, and people.

The New Testament is so countercultural that it doesn't present a mission plan based on money or research. When his disciples asked Jesus, "What about the world?" he told them to love and obey him. "Do what I tell you and the Holy Spirit will do the rest," he said.

However, Jesus was deeply concerned about bugs in the system. The bugs that bothered him the most were the pests that infected the religious leaders among the Pharisees, elders, and chief priests. He persistently bugged them to get rid of their hypocrisy, which was Bug No. 1. They were so buggy that they could not believe Jesus came from God, despite his words and deeds.

Therefore, I suspect that when things go wrong with our church and mission efforts, we need first to check the motives in our own hearts. What kind of bugs do we find there? It's possible for people to be doing mission to earn points with God. People carry on in missionary work out of self-righteous zeal. Outwardly, they show all the signs of success, but inwardly they may be what Jesus called whitewashed sepulchers. The bug of religious phoniness will kill us every time.

Jesus also bugged people to beware of trusting in themselves, their cleverness, their strength, their resources. Beware of where your treasure is, he said, because your heart will follow it.

To get rid of the bugs of materialism, he demanded self-denial and simple faith and trust. Look at the flowers and the sparrows, he said. See how God takes care of them. Therefore, don't worry about things. Don't build your mission plans on your own wisdom, strength, education, training, and money. It's amazing how much church and mission work is consumed by concerns about material things.

Jesus bugged people about pomposity, the desire to be something, the desire to be first. His own team ranted about who were the best players. Even the mother of some of them got involved in jockeying for position. How preposterous. Yet how easy it is to fall into the same trap when we build our plans and organizations. How fraught with spiritual peril when people seek leadership and power for themselves. Let's look for this bug when we ask questions about why we fail in mission.

I'm loading up on bug killers for this summer's battles. It's also time for all of us in world missions to inspect for bug damage. Extermination does not happen by itself. My plea is for internal inspections first. Get the bug out of your own eye, Jesus said, before you judge your brother.

Our vision must be clear. Our love for Jesus must be unalloyed. Our purposes and plans must be guided by his principles. Check his words often and prayerfully, and then spray them over everything you do.

Men: It's time to change

My golfing partner and I sucked in the crisp morning air while we limbered up on the first tee. "Sure beats work," we laughed, getting into high gear for the day, when suddenly appeared—a woman!—obviously prepared to join us for the round. We struggled to keep our inner groans from any outward expression while we exchanged brief pleasantries. But in one devastating moment our chauvinism dissolved as quickly as her drive first exploded and then descended into the luscious fairway turf some 200 yards away.

Change the scene to a packed seminar room, where a visiting missions strategist poured out his new plans for a country suddenly open to Westerners. He unveiled sound ideas for training leaders, an obvious need crying to be met. A certain refrain echoed off the walls: "We'll train so many men here, and we'll train more men in this city, and we have a great opportunity to train men there."

"Men . . . men . . . men . . ." bounced around in my brain as I drove back to the office. How did the women in that room feel? What about the women in that country who need and want training? Why weren't they mentioned? Probably because male prejudice thrived as well in the seminar as it did on the golf course. Ask a missions leader, "Don't women need to be trained?" and his answer would be, "Yes, of course." But look around at the preferences given to men, and listen to our speeches, and read our publicity, and look at our budget allocations, and you'll see that women for the most part are just overlooked and left out of our considerations.

Ignoring women is just as easy as slipping into your car and pulling the lever into drive. Sure, neutral and reverse are important—we couldn't live without them—but they just get in the way of drive. That's exactly how we slight women habitually and unconsciously, all the way from long-range planning to our preaching and writing about world missions.

The needs, potential, and qualifications of women have been shrouded in the mists of interminable squabbles about women's roles in the church. Whatever your view about these matters, our fights have done nothing to erase the deeply ingrained prejudices of men toward women. We cannot continue our rather brutish behavior, thinking that our patient Christian wives, friends, and fellow workers don't really care. We mistakenly assume that because they are not radical feminists they have no feelings.

Change begins with our language, because what we say and what we write reveal our unchallenged assumptions about women. Beyond that, however, we must change our missions commitment to include evangelizing and training the world's women. Women leaders from Africa and Asia have correctly exposed the blind side of church and mission strategies in this regard. If we contemplate new ministries, without taking into account the huge potential for significant leadership among Christian women, we enter the field with one arm cut off.

Too often we act as if missions history means nothing. How many times do we ring the changes on William Carey, Hudson Taylor, and Jim Elliot, without ever mentioning Mary Slessor, Gladys Aylward, and Helen Roseveare? What does such oversight say to women in our schools and churches? If mission work sounds like the private domain of an exclusive men's club, we aren't going to attract capable women.

Perhaps the strongest signal we send to women is the role we give, or do not give, to them in mission leadership. Some of our institutions would be better served if the wives of the men in charge were given the job. In these cases, the wife is gifted in management and administration, while her husband's gifts are teaching, preaching, and counseling. The point is to use people in their strengths, regardless of their sex. The work of God could be considerably expedited if we got serious about developing women for leadership in world missions.

Men, it's long past the time to change.

Theological drift: a noose around the neck of missions

Evangelical educators have been stung by charges that their schools are moving away from orthodoxy. Evangelical mission leaders have been stung by charges that for all their activism, they aren't paying enough attention to their theological roots. The schoolmen are still smarting from a survey of students at 16 colleges and seminaries which showed that they held something less than exuberant convictions on some key doctrinal questions. The man who did the survey and wrote the book (*Evangelicalism: The Coming Generation*, by James Davison Hunter) told a reporter after a recent seminar on the subject that nobody seems to be doing any serious thinking about the theological drift.

The warning to mission leaders came from David Hesselgrave. He wrote: "There is danger that other Evangelicals will take too much for granted and, resting in the security of long-cherished but seldom ree-valuated doctrine, will 'get on' with mission until they belatedly discover that the faith that fueled mission in the first place has eroded away" (*Today's Choices for Tomorrow's Mission*, p. 113).

When you read charges like these, you always wonder if it's time to call the fire department or not. Is our evangelical house going up in flames while we sleep? Are Hunter and Hesselgrave our reliable smoke alarms that we should be jumping out of bed about?

If history tells us anything, it's that theological drift occurs almost imperceptibly over long periods of time. One little change here, another there, and perhaps two or three hundred years later whole institutions and entire denominations have faded into anti-orthodoxy. Take Harvard University and Unitarianism as examples.

In more recent times, schools and mission agencies sworn to orthodoxy think they have built-in protections against what happened to Harvard and the Student Volunteer Movement. They have ironclad doctrinal statements that supposedly can never be changed. But that is a feeble hope at best. History is replete with doctrinal statements that people in those traditions no longer teach or believe.

Another thing is quite certain: Theological drift will eventually put a noose around the neck of world missions, and the mission agencies that fail to pay attention will be left twisting in the wind like a convicted cattle rustler. Some agencies already complain that the schools are to blame for their candidates' theological softness. Some of the schools, in turn, say that the problem isn't theirs, but rather the local church's and the family's. Typical juggling of the hot potato, isn't it?

Wherever the problem starts, mission agencies can't walk away from it. The people they assign to mission tasks must have theological credibility. They cannot risk taking theological cripples and putting them on the field. There is considerable merit to Hesselgrave's warning that our activism—much of it stemming from public relations and financial pressures—will in the end doom us, if we neglect to nurture strong theological convictions. Big numbers and huge successes should never be permitted to mask theological erosion. Perhaps we've glossed over God's lesson to Gideon: We need fewer, but better qualified people, orthodox without slightest hint of theological weakness; living in the power of the Holy Spirit; and tested in the fires of both adversity and homeside experience.

The uncertain trumpet

Hot arguments about the causes of global warming **are once again erupting like a volcano, spewing charges and counter-charges across the scientific community.** What set the ashes and molten lava flowing this time was a document from the United Nations' Intergovernmental Panel on Climate Change. Seems that some of the scientists thought they had said one thing, but the edited report said another. One of them claimed he had never seen a more disturbing corruption of the peer-review process.

This issue goes beyond a little internecine scientific nitpicking, because the U.N. implicates you and me as the cause of global warming. Whatever the report's scientific merits, it will lead to all kinds of new government regulations. Before long, my power-mower will be outlawed, to say nothing of the Freon in my car's air-conditioner. Once again scientists are guilty of sounding a confusing call on their trumpets.

But they are not alone in blowing uncertain notes. Right up there with them are the theologians, Bible scholars, and missiologists. Thinking Christians are thoroughly confused and disgusted by their lack of clarity on the core issue of apostolic concern—we are lost unless we repent and believe the gospel. Then we wonder why people don't give a hoot about sending missionaries. No one has said it better than the apostle Paul: "If the trumpet-call is not clear, who will prepare for battle?"

Lack of clarity has long befuddled the church. Confusion in the ranks stands as Satan's most-loved curse on the church. He knows if Christians quibble about the essentials, passion for missions and evangelism will peter out. If you think Freon is burning a hole in the earth's ozone layer, then these interminable theological disputes are burning holes in plain biblical truth about people being lost apart from faith in Jesus Christ.

The early church and the apostles blew a clear message of hope and salvation because they knew the whole world was in danger of God's righteous judgment. When you start with man's condition (as Paul did in Romans 1-3), you are forced not to look for loopholes but to confess your own guilt before a holy God.

Not a single uncertain note sounded from Paul's trumpet. That's why he was so singularly successful as an evangelist and a church-planting missionary. He did not stop to write a book about the fate of those who never hear. No, he said, everyone is guilty and merits God's righteous judgment. Paul did not have to offer two or three ways for God to work himself out of a theological box of his own making. Only modern scholars try to help God that way.

People who sense that the experts can't agree on either the diagnosis or the remedy for the world's spiritual ills are not likely to jump out of their lawn chairs and head to Nepal and Namibia. (They won't pray and give much, either.)

Now is the time for the church to recapture and reissue a clear call, to lead God's people into worldwide spiritual battles. Forget the debates. Forget the idle speculations of "what if?" Focus on the passion and purpose of the apostles. Reject those who tamper with the written word of God to make it more palatable to modern sensibilities. God's people must be reinvigorated and redirected by some old-fashioned, pulpit-thumping preaching about where all people are headed without Christ, and about the missionary duties of those who profess to believe in him.

The unholy clamor for conversions

One of the miracles of fishing is that fish grow after they're caught. The 10-inch trout in the net becomes a 12-inch trout around the office coffeemaker. Never mind that trout really shrink the longer they're out of the water.

One of the similar miracles of missions is how many thousands of people around the world are converted every year. As Carl Henry once asked, "If we add up all the claims implicit in evangelical promotion, would not the whole world recently have been converted twice over?"

How far we have fallen from the example of the Lord Jesus, who refused to raise a clamor in the streets for his successes. Instead, we now try to out-clamor each other.

This phenomenon usually rises with what we in missions call new opportunities, or open doors. My recollection of it goes back to the end of World War II in Japan, first when Gen. MacArthur appealed for thousands of missionaries, and second when some mission agencies reported thousands of conversions. Nearly half a century later most of Japan remains resolutely non-Christian.

Now it's Russia's turn. The numbers of decisions are staggering. Before that it was Romania and Albania. Before that, many countries in sub-Saharan Africa, plus Korea, Brazil, and Guatemala. (I would include China, except that, mercifully, Western mission boards can't claim credit for thousands, perhaps millions, of conversions there.)

Part of our problem is pragmatic and part theological.

Pragmatically, we have created a public relations and fund-raising monster that must be fed huge numbers. If we're not producing results, the money won't come in. We justify our mission to our supporters by citing spectacular numbers. The numbers may be people who have made decisions, or amounts of relief shipped to starving people, or thousands of pieces of literature printed and distributed, or hundreds of letters received from listeners.

Theologically, we take a huge leap from hands raised, cards signed, or people coming forward, to conversions. Sometimes we try to cover our tracks with such euphemisms as "professed to receive Christ," or "indicated a desire to receive Christ," because we really don't know the true spiritual condition of those who raised their hands, or whatever.

In our haste to accumulate successes we tend not only to become overzealous in claiming more than we should, but we also tend to make it too easy to make a decision in the first place. Dietrich Bonhoeffer called it cheap grace.

Talk to African church leaders and they'll tell you their number one problem is the thousands of unconverted people in their churches. Go to Brazil and ask for a count of the thousands who not only came in the front door of the church, but who soon fled out the back door into the cults. Go to Albania and Romania and look for the thousands of converts who made quick decisions right after the fall of communism. They are not in the churches today. Go to Guatemala where it is evident that much of the evangelical movement is quite cultural.

Now missions are rushing to take advantage not only of political freedom but also of enormous heart hunger in Russia and Ukraine. Hand raisers are spilling out faster than the minuscule number of evangelical churches can absorb them. What will happen to these people after we write home about our successes and, in effect, claim them as new Christians? Will they carve a lasting image in the spiritual contours of Russia? Or will they fade back into their traditional ways, with no one to succor them until they become established members of Christ's body and not just numbers on a press release or mission agency video?

Much more is at stake in world missions than fibbing about numbers of decisions for the sake of good PR. What is at stake is the integrity and health of the indigenous church of Jesus Christ being planted in new soils, the validity of the gospel and Christian doctrine, and the souls of thousands of people who make quick responses to Western appeals, only to fall by the wayside. That's the real tragedy.

Unspeakable affront

The recent discovery of what may turn out to be fossils on Mars sparked a profusion of provocative reactions, not only among scientists but also among religionists and philosophers. One university theologian questioned whether we need "the Jesus story" any more. An editorial writer in *The New Yorker* said that in charting our journey into the future "no Bible will suffice."

About the same time, a Michigan pastor announced to his congregation that Jesus is not the only way to salvation. Fellow pastors denounced him, but most of his parishioners stood up for him. His story also made the *New York Times*.

As surely as Hurricane Fran ravaged North Carolina last month, the world mission of the church is under assault. The attacks come from outside and inside. We have no mission if the Jesus story is unnecessary; we have no mission if any sincere religionist can get to heaven without confessing Christ as Lord and Savior.

Yet little is being done to answer these remarkable threats to our mission. Apologetics seems about as respected in world missions today as my old MacPlus computer. Somehow, our defenses seem to have evaporated in the mists of being nice to everybody. Political and cultural respect now require us to admit everybody to God's heaven, no matter whether they are legitimate ticketholders or not.

Why bother mounting missionary apologetics? After all, we're on a roll, aren't we? Look how evangelicalism has exploded globally in the last half-century. "We're winning!" we shout.

Perhaps, but we haven't crossed the goal line yet. I suppose the Christians across the Middle East, Eastern Europe, and North Africa thought they had the game all wrapped up between A.D. 300 and 400, didn't they? What do you find there today? Dusty, rock-strewn, weed-overgrown ruins of once glorious, packed out churches. Why? When false religion advanced, they were dead meat.

We are never in more danger than when we forget about the enemies waiting to devour us on the outskirts of town. The devil has cleverly worked overtime as an angel of light to create false philosophies and religions. I don't think anyone, no matter how sincere, will find salvation in any of these systems. If we do not attack these intellectual and religious challenges head-on, we will look around one day and wonder what happened to our missionary vision.

Missionary theologians must remind us of the truth of the gospel. They must reaffirm not only that the Jesus story is absolutely essential, but that it excludes all other religious stories as valid paths to eternal salvation. We need the apostolic passion of Ephesians 1: We are blessed with every spiritual blessing in Christ. We are adopted as God's sons through Christ. We have redemption and the forgiveness of sins in Christ. God is bringing all things together under one head, even Christ. This is not only Christ-centered doctrine, it is exclusively Christ's. Can you imagine substituting any other name in this text?

Let us be gripped by Paul's unassailable dogmatism, without queasiness. If our world mission means anything, it means the powerful proclamation that no other name, philosophy, religion, scientific world view, or whatever, is ever going to bring anyone salvation. Never.

To say that a sincere Protestant, Catholic, Jew, Orthodox, Hindu, Muslim, Buddhist, Taoist, or animist is going to gain salvation apart from confessing Jesus Christ as Lord and Savior is an unspeakable affront to his blood.

When will the sun set on racism?

Sir Francis Younghusband was knighted not for converting Tibet but for conquering it. In the end, however, Tibet conquered him. Not by military force, of course, but by the power of its Buddhist mysticism. Sir

Francis, the impulsive imperial soldier, turned guru.

After Younghusband's arrogant, needless expedition in 1904, during which his troops massacred pathetically outgunned Tibetans, he wrung concessions from them that went far beyond his government's instructions. As he was leaving, the Tibetans gave Younghusband a bronze statue of the Buddha, which he treasured for the rest of his life.

Sir Francis (1863-1942) breathed the late 19th century air of colonialism and racial superiority. He thought he was doing the "Oriental races" a favor when he invaded them, because they were "not a fit people to be left to themselves." Never mind that Tibet's Dalai Lama preferred not to be included in Britain's empire.

But his encounter with Tibetan Buddhists left him feeling that their civilization was spiritually superior to his own. It also gave him a second career, so to speak, which he pursued with the same vengeance and dedication that had marked his military accomplishments. Zealously he wrote books on religious self-realization. He even suggested to the woman in his life that they produce a "God Child" who would be "greater even than Jesus." This idea, his biographer Patrick French writes, "was an extension of the optimistic idealism that had enabled him to believe in the value of colonial rule as a doctrine of compassion."

The modern missionary movement blossomed in the same cultural environment, as missionaries kept hot on the heels of British, French, and German soldiers wherever they went in Africa and Asia. Colonialism was their protective shield. They, too, saw "the value of colonial rule as a doctrine of compassion." Missionary correspondence reveals strong feelings that the "natives" were not fit to be left to themselves.

Of course, missionary compassion also included preaching the gospel, establishing schools and hospitals, and building churches. Their remarkable, courageous, and sacrificial endeavors must never be negated by prevailing colonial and racist attitudes. It's far too easy for us to remember their faults and forget how many of them gave their lives and the lives of their children for the sake of Jesus.

But what does Sir Francis tell us today? I see some startling similarities in the number of educated Westerners who fall under the sway of Eastern mysticism. Missionaries armed with notions of Western superiority march into spiritual battles totally unprepared for the enemy's power in Hinduism and Buddhism. We are tragically naive about their ability to conquer us. We don't even recognize what these religions are doing to America, let alone how they devour even some of the best-intentioned, but often misguided, missionaries.

The second message Sir Francis sends is that yes, even today, we Christians (including some missionaries) have not totally eradicated colonial snobbery toward people in other countries. We still harbor a strong Messiah-complex, which often motivates our missions. Obviously, we are better, or we would not be delivering so much help and spending so many millions of dollars.

Of course, we're not as brash about it as Sir Francis and his peers were, but the residue of racial and spiritual superiority clings to us and stinks like cow manure. The sun has long set on the British Empire, but the last rays of racism have yet to sink below the horizon. Perhaps that's one reason we don't see more spiritual fruit from our labors, both in the U.S. and overseas.

Why are there no women on the panel?

There she was, gracing the front page of the *New York Times*—Pakistan's Prime Minister Benazir Bhutto—answering questions from the press with President Clinton. What a striking contrast, I thought, with the setting about a month earlier at a missions conference. On that occasion I sat, not with President Clinton, but with eight of my peers answering questions every afternoon.

The audience, mostly missionaries, peppered us with the toughest questions you can imagine. On the last afternoon one of them asked, "Why are there no women on the panel? Women do make up two-thirds of the missionary force." We felt as if we had been caught with our hands in the cookie jar. Were there no Benazir Bhuttos among us? No women qualified to sit on a panel of "experts"?

That scene leads to a few observations. First, this simple, heartfelt question resembles many others that have been asked countless times in silence, but rarely openly at missionary gatherings, on the field, and at home. Questions about women's roles do not necessarily come from radicals trying to force a feminist takeover of the missions establishment. People trying to rewrite the Bible to fit current cultural norms are not responsible for all of the questions. To often we dismiss questions about women's roles as the work of liberal rabble-rousers. Too often we try to avoid facing the questions, challenging our attitudes, and seeing whether we need to change our ways.

Second, all of us good guys on the panel wore white hats. That is, we did not decide prior to the conference that no women would sit on the panel with us. It was just naturally assumed—with no intentional slights or malice toward any women—that our panel of experts would be comprised of men.

Those kinds of assumptions strike at the core of our thinking about leadership, management, supervisory, and board roles for women in missions. Male leaders are good people, but we just don't get the point about women's aspirations, and how our unintentional slights often produce deep hurts and, sometimes, lifelong scars. To say nothing of how we have shortchanged ourselves and our ministries by not even thinking about the spiritual endowments of women, and the tremendous good they could do for us, our ministries, and our organizations if we only encouraged them to do so.

I would love to know what Euodia and Syntyche did as co-missionaries with the apostle Paul. He called them his fellow workers who had "contended" with him, or shared his struggles, "in the cause of the gospel." (I don't care for the NIV's "contended," because it smacks too much of argument.) Perhaps they did nothing more or less than the thousands of other women down through the centuries who have charted the course for evangelism, church growth, and discipleship around the world.

On the other hand, I'm not content with such an implied limit on their roles. In fact, I see no limits to their responsible authority and leadership in mission. Paul appears not to have placed any restrictions on Priscilla.

But we have, in effect, said to women missionaries, "you can do whatever you want to do, except . . . ." We do not baldly state our exceptions, but they are part of the often unwritten ethos of many boards. No, we prove our exceptions by what we do not do—give women missionaries management staff positions.

Of course, not every woman missionary wants to be a manger, but many do, and they feel denied the opportunity for professional advancement and spiritual ministry on increasingly higher levels of responsibility. I salute the courageous few who serve in what often seems like token roles. But when are we going to admit our biases—even the unconscious ones—and confess that we have needlessly hurt and suppressed capable, spiritually gifted women?

Women who have made a difference

In September, the world honored two women, a princess and a nun, for what each one had done in her own way to alleviate human suffering.

Princess Diana raised considerable sums because her station in life allowed her to draw attention to what she believed in; Mother Teresa inspired thousands of volunteers to care for the poor, sick, and dying because she herself did it.

The accolades of praise and the honors and tributes that followed their deaths reminded me of how much better the world is because of the countless number of women who have decided to make a difference, and not be content to leave the world the same as it was when they were born. I'm not thinking just of those women whose exploits are duly recorded in our history books. Florence Nightingale, Catherine Booth, Susan B. Anthony, and Frances Willard—to name a few—have been recognized as world-changing women.

But too often, it seems to me, we have lost sight of how women have made a powerful difference, and they are still doing it without the fanfare of trumpets and drums to call attention to their deeds. As I watched the magnificent service in Westminster Abbey for Princess Diana, I recalled some of the heroines of the church's world mission who easily could have deserved the same kind of farewell. I thought of Lottie Moon, who made such a difference in China; of Amy Carmichael, who in her own way touched India as much as Mother Teresa has; of Mary Slessor, who changed southern Nigeria.

Their names cause barely a ripple today, but every time I read about their mighty exploits of faith I thank God for their selfless dedication and courage. They touched lives for Jesus in such dramatic ways that we shake our heads in unbelief. How did they do it? we wonder.

Lest I be accused of living in the past, let me remind you that pages of mission history are being written today by women just like Lottie Moon, Amy Carmichael, and Mary Slessor. Some of their stories are breaking into print already. Lorry Lutz has written a compelling book, *Women as Risk-Takers for God*, about contemporary women who have done remarkable deeds (World Evangelical Fellowship).

Of course, these women have not followed Jesus to hear people tell them how great they are. They have followed Jesus because they love him and want to touch others with his love. The knowledge of Christ around the world would be greatly diminished if not for the love, tenderness, dedication, sacrifice, and suffering of missionary women.

To me, it's a disgrace to see responsible church and mission leaders bickering over women's roles, when we all know full well what women have done, can do, and will do for the cause of Christ. Take the women out of church and mission, and we would be as stalemated in the battle for souls as Napoleon was in the snow at the gates of Moscow.

Before the last hurrahs for Princes Diana and Mother Teresa float away, let's roll the drums and blow the trumpets for all the women soldiers of the cross who have fought the good fight of faith on the world's toughest battlegrounds. We must honor today's contingent with our prayers, encouragement, and enablement, so they can achieve their God-given visions without any ungodly hindrances from the male side of God's family.

The Missionary Life

Do families still fit in missions?

Missionary recruiters understandably are perplexed by would-be missionaries who insist that their families come first. Or, as an older missionary complained, "Jesus isn't Lord; the family is." Not too long ago it was assumed that one price of being a missionary was the sacrifice of your family. Now the pendulum has swung the other way. As a seminary-trained man recently insisted to me, "Jesus never said we should leave our wives and children." Really? What about, "No one who has left home or brothers or sisters or mother or father or children or fields for me . . ."?

This issue forces missions leaders to walk a tightrope across Niagara Falls. First, they have to acknowledge that the past record of world missions reveals some disgraceful treatment of wives, children, parents, and grandparents. On the other hand, they have to stand against some popular teaching that seems to put family welfare ahead of everything else in the kingdom.

Not only are missions recruiters, teachers, and pastors in a jam, so are the young husbands and wives contemplating careers in missions. Gurus bombard them with generalities about the faults of boarding schools. They claim that you're worse than an infidel if you don't educate your children at home.

These young couples feel like batter freshly poured into a waffle iron. They're taking heat from both the family-first camp and the missions camp. Consequently, we're losing some talented people from the cause of world evangelization. Right now the family supremacy movement appears to be eclipsing the missions movement.

The cause of missions is also hurt by inflexible attitudes among missions leaders who don't realize that today's young people have been thoroughly sensitized about family issues and job expectations. We cannot go on giving the impression that if you take your family seriously you really aren't dedicated to Christ and ready to be a missionary.

Adjustments have to be made on both sides, to avoid situations where successful workers have been so overworked that they have had to resign and take secular jobs, just so they can have adequate time with their families. Finding the balance between ministry and family will always be as difficult as Solomon's decision between the two mothers claiming the same baby.

Young couples' perplexity could be alleviated if the family experts would come down a peg from Mount Sinai, and stop dumping guilt on young families who are willing to accept the cost of some painful family separations for the sake of the gospel. Additionally, missions recruiters could be more user-friendly and refuse to make a career in missions an either-or proposition. Legitimate concerns of young couples must be addressed sympathetically, not judgmentally.

Above all, we must insist on the compelling supremacy of Christ's lordship. We can't simply throw out the New Testament teaching about self-denial and sacrifice. Working as a missionary overseas is not the same as doing a comfortable job at home, so we must not be surprised that some highly qualified people will turn aside from missions, like the rich young ruler, because of the cost. We must be honest enough to say that serving Jesus Christ overseas will make unusual, severe demands on the family's faith, strength, and resilience.

However, we must also make absolutely clear that a missions career does not necessarily have to wreck the family. More than enough resources are available in the missions community to build good marriages and satisfying relationships between parents and children. Field leaders must make family unity and stability a high priority. Isn't Jesus Christ strong enough to keep us on the missionary firing line, while at the same time giving us a wonderfully satisfying family life?

"Have I told you lately that I love you?"

Somehow, miraculously, I escaped the sandman's shroud last night while watching the late news. I used to wonder how my dad could possibly fall asleep during the news; now I do it myself every night. But not last night. I watched them disentangle the wreckage of a small plane that crashed in Wyoming, and listened to people argue whether a 7-year-old girl should have been allowed to fly the plane across the country. Next, the usual expose of corruption in Chicago.

Somewhere down the line came one of those 30-second segments that hardly qualify as news, but these days any medical discovery seems to be worth reporting. Guess what? Perhaps you've already known, but my brain has shrunk. Since this phenomenon only applies to males, we were told, it helps to explain why old men are grumpy.

Grumpy or not, there are some things that pop up in

my brain that I would like to get rid of but can't. How can the scientists explain, for example, why suddenly, from out of nowhere, I recalled that old, old ballad, "Have I told you lately that I love you?"

Why is that refrain ricocheting around my cranium? Of course, I thought first about telling my wife, Martha, but I already had. (We had made a pact when we were married that never would a day pass without our telling each other, "I love you.") But then I wondered, How often do we tell our missionaries overseas that we love and appreciate them? I had to confess that I don't do it often enough.

We faithfully send our support checks; they are processed by the home office, and we get a thank-you note with our receipt. Perhaps if we were allowed to send our checks directly to our missionaries, we would tell them how grateful we are for their lives and sacrificial service for the Lord Jesus. But we can't do that if we want a receipt to verify our income tax deductions.

What can we do to rectify this oversight? "Have I told you lately that I love you?" inspired me to designate this week as NATIONAL MISSIONARY APPRECIATION WEEK. Convene a special missionary appreciation night at your church. Don't challenge anybody to do anything except say Thank You to their missionaries. Start with the children. Celebrate with drawings, verses, photos, songs. Write special words to a familiar tune for the kids.

If any of your missionaries are in town, invite them. Toast them and have a party afterwards. Don't ask them to speak—just listen to your words of love and appreciation. Every family should say, "I love you," in a card for at least one missionary family. Read some of these notes to the congregation. Ask two or three people to tell something about their particular missionary family that they appreciate. Video the whole service and send it to your missionaries.

Use the celebration to remind people that missionaries need to hear words of love, gratitude, and appreciation regularly. Ask people to write at least a quarterly love letter. The best time to do this is when the missionaries send you their prayer letter and thank-you notes for your prayers and support.

My brain may be shrinking, but I hope it keeps on telling me what I need to do. "Have I told you lately that I love you" tells me that we love our missionaries for who they are, not primarily for what they do. Do it today. Tell them you love them.

The Epaphroditus Corps

Because of political and economic uncertainties, as well as religious rivalries, missionaries live on the edge. Security is a scarce commodity. They can't bank on everything humming along peacefully day after day. They live the New Testament pictures of the Christian life that most of us only talk about in Sunday school.

When a crisis turns the country upside down, they ask: Shall we stay or go? What about our children? What about our house? Our belongings? How much can we take with us? If we go, where shall we stay, and for how long?

Those are decisions we faced in 1979 when the Three Mile Island nuclear plant near Harrisburg, Pa., malfunctioned, to put it mildly. As with catastrophes overseas, nobody seemed to know the truth, and we—along with thousands of others—were left hanging in limbo. But those of us living within a certain distance of the plant were told to prepare to evacuate. I said, "Let's take our credit cards and get out of here." But my wife wanted to collect family mementos. As it turned out, we didn't have to pack up and leave. I preached on fear the next Sunday and the response was remarkable. Some people came to faith in Christ.

Last year some of our friends decided to evacuate a certain country, especially because the wife was seven months pregnant. They prayed and God sent someone to watch their house. After their arrival in the States, their baby was born without any complications. That was big, of course, but God also poured out a multitude of additional special blessings: missionary-in-residence service at their church; graduate school classes; housing (three rooms for a family of four, but a place to live all the same); a car, computer, and closets full of clothes for themselves and their two boys. They departed from the field with two suitcases, but God has met all of their needs.

God did not drop all of these things out of the sky like a gigantic UPS delivery. They came through the kindness, generosity, and care of fellow Christians. This family's story demonstrates missionary partnership at its best. Missionary service is first and foremost partnership and fellowship in the gospel. This is what inspired the apostle Paul when he thanked the Philippians for the part they played in the work of the gospel.

The Christians who helped our missionary friends belonged to the Epaphroditus Corps. The Philippians commissioned one of their own church members,

Epaphroditus, to minister to Paul's needs. In so doing, the man risked his life to render to Paul the service the Philippians could not give in person. Paul knew that through Christ he had the strength for anything, but he confessed that he received Christ's strength through what the Philippians had done for him.

The Philippians sent money, of course, which Paul accepted as a fragrant offering and acceptable sacrifice, pleasing to God. But they also sent Epaphroditus to care for their missionary. Our partnerships with our missionaries must include our money and our people. God has a place for every Christian in his missionary program. Some he calls to do the work of an apostle, evangelist, and church planter, like Paul. Some he calls to serve the needs of missionaries, like Epaphroditus.

Perhaps we could enlist many more people in missions if we held out the vision of the Epaphroditus Corps. People like him are needed not just for emergency evacuations, but for the daily encouragement, prayer, and fellowship all missionaries desire. Who will be the next Epaphroditus your church sends to care for a missionary?

Fortified missionaries

Which is worse, Super Bowl hype or cereal bowl hype? Mercifully, Super Bowl hype lasts only two weeks, but cereal bowl hype goes on and on and on like that pink rabbit beating the bass drum for Eveready batteries.

Critics complain there's too much sugar in the cereal bowl hype, but the manufacturers say they stuff their products with vitamins, minerals, and other essential nutrients. I'm sorry, I should not have said "stuff," because actually they use a much more sophisticated word: their cereals are "fortified."

Doesn't that make you feel much stronger? Aren't you raring to take on the world's challenges after you've been fortified with breakfast cereal?

Well, yes. Actually, a lot of what we eat and drink has been fortified with an amazing array of substances designed to ward off deficiencies of various kinds and build stronger bodies. If I had to choose, I'd rather be fortified than malnourished.

The same principle holds in my love affair with Jesus Christ. I would much rather be fortified by him than stagger through life on short rations. Think of that the next time you pray for your missionaries. Ask God to fortify them.

Of course, when Jesus fortifies us he expects to see something for the vitamins and minerals he pumps into us. He does not fortify us just so we can be as fat and sleek as a 4-H champion baby beef. He wants us to be so well-nourished that we will engage in successful ventures to advance his cause, not ours.

The church and its missionaries are fortified by Jesus as they conduct his agenda to bring people to trust, love, and obey him. The apostle Paul prayed that the church would be fortified "in every good deed and word." No act or word is insignificant if it is infused with Christ's power.

Just as we gather around our loaded cereal bowls in the morning, slurping up our daily quota of vitamins and minerals, so our missionaries need a daily dose of Christ's nourishment. Therefore, our morning bowl of corn flakes or bran flakes—depending on your age—should remind us to pray for our friends as they engage enemy strongholds around the world. Jesus promised to nourish his church, not once a week, or once a day, but all the time.

God calls the church to bear witness to the gospel "in every good word and deed." If we are to see the light gain against the darkness, each personal word and deed must be fortified by the Holy Spirit. After all, he is the supreme energizer. Nothing happens without him.

It's a scary thought, but we have to be absolutely certain that our mission efforts have not been stripped of essential nutrients. Just as it is possible to fill up on empty calories, and think you're doing your body some good, so it's possible to run around the world and promote a flurry of activity that looks good, but is devoid of the life of Jesus.

We cannot take such a gamble. Being fortified by Jesus sounds like tame activity. Rather like stroking a kitten than challenging a lion with a broom and a chair. But Jesus flatly said that without him we can do absolutely nothing. Zero. Zip. Zilch.

He is the vine and we are the branches. Unless vital nutrients flow from the vine and fortify the branches, no fruit will appear—no good deeds and no good words. Not only that, such branches will be lopped off.

The next time you watch a cereal pitchman on TV, check your intake of Christ's vitamins and minerals, and pray for your missionary friends to be fortified by him.

Missionaries need heart

After 16 years of tough work, the late Ray Buker left Burma in 1942 in the face of oncoming Japanese troops. That wasn't the end, however, because he came home zealous to stir up missionary vision and passion wherever he went. He stirred up Baptists to start their own conservative mission board. He stirred up students while teaching missions at Denver Seminary. At age 68 he began to stir up a lot of missionaries to start training leaders by using extension programs. Ray kept on stirring up people until he died at 92.

Ray exhorted, but he did not agitate. He did not make a pest of himself. We all respected him and listened to him not just because he was a friendly, outgoing guy with a quick smile. We listened because his integrity compelled us to. Not a smidgeon of phoniness marred his character. His record of deeds done stands out like Mount Rushmore on the South Dakota plains.

The writer of Hebrews desperately needed a team of Ray Bukers. Ray, by the way, ran in the 1924 Olympics. Those first readers of Hebrews were a dispirited gaggle of straggling runners—not in the Olympics but in the far tougher race to glory. They had weak knees and feeble arms, among other things. Few of them appeared to be stripped for action, going flat out to win. Others dawdled along, complaining how tough the race was. Some slipped dangerously close to the edge of the track, and some had turned cold (they had "hard hearts") and quit.

"Encourage one another to keep going," the writer of Hebrews pleaded. Ray Buker was an encourager par excellence. Sadly, however, our Christian culture has diluted the word "encourage." Give him a pat on the back, we say, and that's about it. More accurately, it seems to me, we ought to say, "Come on, brother, get moving."

The classic first definition of courage is "the heart, as the seat of intelligence or of feeling; hence, mind, spirit, temper, or disposition."

To encourage people means to put heart into them. That's what our missionaries need—heart. Their needs lists always include many things like health, results in ministry, good relations, learning the language and culture, adequate support, housing, and good schools for their children. But more than anything else they need hearts of lions.

We can't provide heart transplants, but we can do what the writer of Hebrews tells us, "Encourage one another daily . . . so that none of you may be hardened by sin's deceitfulness" (3:13). Dodging a fatal heart attack is the key to missionary perseverance. Sin (personalized as the enemy) tricks missionaries and they fall victim to hard hearts—mainly dissension and discouragement (which take the heart out of them). To prevent this they need a daily shot of heart-strengthening encouragement.

We can put heart into them by calling, faxing, writing, and sending boxes of goodies. We ought to take them out to dinner when we travel to their places on business and vacation trips. While there, we ought to listen to them for a couple of hours. We can put their minds at ease so they don't have to worry about their support or their kids' education. We can give them an annual cost-of-living raise.

We can put heart into them by sending our pastors to

visit them. They need our regular counsel, exhortation, inspiration, and stimulation. Above all, however, we must encourage missionaries with fervent, informed prayer.

That's all long-distance heart pumping. Who are the encouragers on the battlefield? On my overseas trips, I've always been thankful to receive appreciation for bringing encouragement. But I wonder why missionaries seem to spend so little time putting heart into each other. Heart building does not get the priority it needs. If they are going to win the faith race, missionaries must be Ray Bukers to each other, lest they give up and quit.

Missionary warfare

The other night I stumbled on to "The Guns of Navarone," a classic World War II film about how some undercover agents sabotaged a Nazi battery that was taking dead aim on an incoming flotilla of British ships. Of course, as in any gripping war novel, the Germans captured the gang of saboteurs. They interrogated them, trying to find out where they had hidden their explosives, and then threatened to torture them. However, the heroes escaped and completed their hair-raising mission.

Unfortunately, interrogation and torture are not limited to old war movies, even though those of us safely ensconced under the umbrella of freedom too often assume they are. They are part of the war raging between the powers of darkness and the Lord Jesus. The enemy seizes every opportunity to throttle the good news of the gospel. Many times missionaries, as well as local believers, are called in for questioning because they are assumed to be threats to the spiritual enemy's strongholds of darkness. The ultimate enemy controls these countries by combining religious and political power.

I recalled the interrogation scene from the movie when I read the first-hand account of a missionary's interrogation in a North African country. This country's security apparatus was so zealous that its agents nailed the missionary on the ship before he landed. He was in their computers as an undesirable, so he was told to report to the police when he arrived at his destination.

He was interrogated twice the next week, but not tortured. The issue boiled down to what he was doing in the country, the meetings of Christians in his house, and the possibility that he was bribing people to convert. He was warned not to coerce anyone into becoming a Christian by material means. His case is pending. Previously, the police had seized all his books and videos.

In many countries, hostility to the gospel is rampant. Local Christians and missionaries are routinely called in for questioning. Religious freedom is a fiction.

We would like to believe that all countries respect the United Nations Charter, but when their national faith is at stake they will take whatever means necessary to protect it. Being a citizen of the United States carries no weight at all, and in some places is a hindrance to gospel witness.

What recourse do we have? Shall we give up the fight? Shall we shake the dust off our feet and move on to the next country? To give up would be to deny the missionary heart of our faith. It will also amount to an admission that the gospel has lost its power. Is Jesus stronger than Islam, or is he not?

Among our primary needs, we must be sure the people we send into warfare are prepared. Countries like this one are no place for people with little or no experience witnessing to people of other faiths.

For example, during the wait for police questioning the missionary was able to discuss with his guard the essentials of salvation by faith alone and the wonder of God's love. He read to him from Ephesians 2:8, 9 and John 3:16-20. He explained that this is what he does with the people of the country. People believe on their own, not because he pays them.

We also need to pray like we are at war. The church is at war. We have to believe and act on what Paul said: "We do not wage war according to human standards; for the weapons of our warfare are not merely human, but they have divine power to destroy strongholds" (2 Cor. 10:3, 4). That's what missionary work is all about, and if we are to win, every Christian must join the fight.

The home crowd advantage

What's the home crowd advantage worth? Coaches and athletes won't put a price tag on it, but they claim it's significant. Once in a while you'll even see a player actually gesturing to the crowd to "get into it" and whoop it up some more. Even multimillion-dollar performers still need the home folks to inspire them to even greater efforts to win.

What about our missionaries, who get considerably less? Do they need the home folks to start the "wave," or something like that, to raise their flagging spirits and cheer them on to even greater levels of dedication and service? Yes, of course they do, because they're human beings like the rest of us, and they need to know there's a crowd pushing them to smash home runs and rip off double plays, so to speak.

Because it's biblical, too. "So go on cheering and strengthening each other," the apostle Paul told the Thessalonians (1 Thess. 5:11, Phillips). In the case of missions, the home folks ought to be the cheering section for the people on the front lines. Pretend you're in the grandstand at your favorite stadium, screaming your lungs out, and translate that into what you can do to hearten and fortify your missionary friends.

A booming yell lets the players know you're awake and on their side. Try that on your missionaries, because many of them never hear from you from one year to the next, and they wonder if you are in the same stadium they are. They fight loneliness and depression, and, worse, the fear that the folks have forgotten or deserted them.

Get your lungs cranked up and let them hear from you regularly. Send your cheers by phone, fax, or mail, but deluge them with cheers like they are champions parading through the city after winning the World Series.

"We love you! We love you! We love you!" won't be heard at your neighborhood ballyard, but that's what our missionary players need to hear from their cheering section. Followed by, "We pray for you! We pray for you! We pray for you!" That's the hometown advantage.

Those are our persistent cheers. But they also need some unexpected cheers to punctuate the special days, things like birthdays and anniversaries. Find some creative cheers. Do a little research on what would be especially appreciated, a nice check for dinner out and enough to pay for the babysitter, for example. Perhaps some perfume that's too expensive where they work, or even something ordinary that we take for granted but they can't afford.

Cheers that make a difference come from people who show serious interest in what the players are doing. This is a plea for informed cheering. Show missionaries you want to dig beyond the superficial stuff. Nothing cheers up a missionary more than a letter asking for more details about the country, the people, politics, economics, poverty, the ministry, the daily grind. It's especially heartening to ask, "How can we help you? What do you need?"

If this kind of unrelenting cheering goes on while our people are on the field, they won't feel like unwelcome intruders when they come home. A Bronx cheer to those who give phony cheers when the missionary gets his "two-minute update" Sunday morning after being away four years.

Our heartfelt cheers can assure them they are deeply appreciated for who they are as much as for the work they do. Very infrequently, if ever, does the crowd cheer one of their own Major League hitters when he strikes out, but it happened the other night. Why? Because he "hung tough," as the sportscasters say, and fought off the pitcher's best stuff for a long time before he took his final whiff. They cheered his character.

"We love you, we pray for you, we appreciate you." Our missionaries need to hear this. The home crowd advantage won't amount to much if all it means is a monthly receipt notice from the board. For too long we've sent people to fight our battles without sending our cheers.

The perils and blessings of singleness

Over the past quarter century, I've watched a little **girl grow in Christ, in the church, and in Christian service in a tough urban setting.** I've watched her with delight, thanksgiving, and praise to God. She has excelled in ministry and in godly character. But, in the eyes of some, she's defective because she is single.

"I don't understand why you're not married yet," some friends tell her. She interprets this as, "Well, obviously there must be something wrong with you."

This is a burden she really doesn't understand, but unfortunately she and many, many other women missionaries carry it every day. It's ironic that while we support them, pray for them, and cheer them on in their work, we slap them down and make them feel like lepers. On the field, often they find equal treatment as illusory as a desert mirage.

As I read my missionary letters and look at my world map, I am overwhelmed by the single women I can name who have taken on highly significant roles in making Jesus known and in serving his people. Some I have worked closely with, with great appreciation for their skills, their witness, and their Christlikeness. Each has worked through the painful issue of singleness in her own way, without acting like a martyr.

We have to recognize that, in addition to all of the other ministry responsibilities they carry, they also live with the stigma of singleness. Rather than add to their difficulties with our insensitive questions, we should pray for them to receive the unique love of Jesus reserved for them.

Thank God that week in and week out women enter missionary service for the first time. However, many have not yet resolved the issue of their singleness. They are encouraged to deal with it during prefield counseling, but, like a nagging backache, it rarely goes away. On the field, away from family and friends, the longing for companionship intensifies. They need trusted friends with whom they can talk freely. What they don't need are aspersions from friends who think they must find a man.

Answers don't come overnight, especially for young women. They find it hard to admit their struggle. The woman whose missionary career I have followed closely is now in her 30s. She has faced her singleness with spiritual aplomb and courage.

Drawing upon an analogy from professional sports, she says that she is God's "free agent" holding out for his best offer. In the meantime, she's playing hard on this "free agent" team. Should the time come for marriage, she'll be ready.

But what about the perils of singleness? She admits that she has spent too many years and too much of her time and energy wistfully looking at the "greener grass," to the neglect of her personal growth and focus in ministry.

The blessings? Foremost, she knows this is God's intention for her life at this time. Beyond that, she knows she could not have done what she has done in ministry for the past 10 years had she been married. She knows she could not have lived as biculturally as she has. Bottom line: "I thank God for my singleness."

As we pray for our single women missionary friends,

we must bring to God this aspect of their lives. Pray for more than the work they do. Pray that they will not keep looking at the "greener grass" to the neglect of their own walk with Christ and their ministry focus. Pray that they will know how to handle those who unthinkingly ask them why they aren't married. These women are so essential to what God is doing around the world that we must not lose them to the perils of their singleness.

The subtle killer: busyness

How would you like to cover commencement speeches for the *New York Times*? Imagine trying to pick a few choice quotes out of a 30-minute address, because each speaker (unless it's President Bush or Gen. Schwarzkopf) gets only two or three paragraphs. That's like trying to eliminate all of your pizza toppings except one or two.

In the May 21 "Commencements" column in the *Times*, I learned that Seton Hall University graduates were told to be aware of intolerance and prejudice; Mannes College of Music graduates were told to rise to the defense of the arts. And, imagine this, Boston College grads were warned that busyness crowds out God's voice. Not your typical send-off, to be sure.

Timothy Healy, president of the New York Public Library, nailed the DANGER label on busyness: "The more one is drawn into the maelstrom of human doing, the more one's days and nights are preoccupied by the sheer busyness of living, the more distant becomes the 'still small voice.'" That "still small voice," of course, was

God's. Elijah, who had just decimated the ranks of the prophets of Baal, heard it.

I don't know what those Boston College people thought, but I wondered how much of our missions business could accurately be described as "preoccupation with the sheer busyness of living." In our work for the Lord, is his voice becoming more distant, or does it ring through with compelling clarity?

We are alarmed by the forces of evil that seem to be screaming across our horizons like some terribly dark and fearsome funnel cloud of an approaching tornado. We agonize with the disasters that befall hundreds of thousands of people, most of them perishing without the least glimmer of hope. We despair over the powerful infusions of power into resurgent anti-Christian religions.

But none of that seems to budge us from our deeply entrenched habits—the busyness of living—that like leeches suck the vitality from our missionary work.

In the home office, busyness means an interminable round of paper shuffling. On the field, busyness means going to the store, fixing the car, picking up the mail, doing the laundry, cooking meals, writing prayer letters, filling out reports, standing in line to get papers for one thing or the other, caring for sick kids, and sitting through hours and hours of "business" meetings with other missionaries.

Where in all of this does the so-called real work of missions happen? Where in the midst of all of these time-consumers do we hear God's still, small voice?

It's terribly easy—and fatal—to equate busyness with spirituality, or with doing something significant in world missions. That's like equating months of painstaking preparation for a space shuttle flight with the flight itself.

If we miss God's voice in our home offices and in our field work, we miss everything in world missions. Waiting for his voice is not a luxury to be squeezed into a hectic flurry of work. No, waiting for and hearing God's voice is the critical element, before which everything else must take a back seat. If we miss his voice because of our busyness with good, important, essential duties, we have missed everything. Like Martha, we have fussed over the kitchen and missed the exquisite pleasure of sitting with Jesus.

Those we leave behind

Starting out for the mission field, for some people at least, is like stepping into a rubber raft headed down the Colorado River gorge through the Grand Canyon. But when they finally depart, they do so not only with their heavenly Father's protection, but also with the prayers of a wide circle of friends.

Meanwhile, what about those they leave behind, their immediate families, their parents and grandparents? Are they not also headed down the Colorado River in a rubber raft? Certainly. This is totally new territory for them, but who prays for them? Who helps them understand what life is like on the mission field?

The father of a missionary about to leave for a certain country asked me if it was safe for him and his wife to visit. He knew I had been there several times. He also knew, from what he had seen on television, that this was a dangerous part of the world, teeming with terrorists.

He was a well-educated, successful businessman, but the images he had seen on television had created a monstrous caricature of the people his son and daughter-in-law were going to serve. In his mind, they were all bad, dangerous, and hardly the kind of people you'd want to spend your vacation with.

Admittedly, the needs of missionaries' parents, siblings, and grandparents rank about as high on our needs scale as cleaning our gutters. We only do it when the water starts pouring over the sides and seedlings start to sprout in the residue of last fall's leaves.

Those whom our missionaries leave behind are left behind in more ways than mere distance. When we pray for missionaries over there, we usually forget to pray for those over here. Unfortunately, because of our lack in this regard, some crisis more serious than loneliness and worry can set in. Some families have harbored bitterness and resentment for years because their children have gone to the mission field. Others, trying to avoid the pain, have deliberately tried to prevent their children from going at all.

Into whose care shall we commit those we leave behind? Obviously, the primary duty lies with the children who have gone to the field. They need to be extremely sensitive to the needs of their parents and grandparents at this juncture. In addition to praying for them, they need to write, call, and fax frequently, and send lots of pictures and videos, especially if they have children. They need to realize how unsettling TV news can be, and go the extra mile to assure their parents of their safety.

Pastors and church missions committees must work better to develop strong support links for those we leave behind. It would be great if once every six months all of these folks could get together, talk about their children and grandchildren, swap pictures, discuss their fears, and pray. They must also talk about the distortions they can get from three-second news clips on TV, and how they can get more accurate foreign news.

Mission boards, too, need to do all they can to reassure those left behind that their children are in good hands, especially when a crisis erupts overseas. Someone in the home office should be designated as the prime communicator to this special part of the mission's larger support family. The mission's mailing list could be segmented, and those left behind could receive an occasional insider's newsletter with information about how to cope with long absences from one's children and grandchildren.

Those we leave behind are not looking for medals for bravery, but they do need to know their sacrifices are appreciated and that they are surrounded by the strong encouragement and support of their missionary children, their churches, and their mission boards.

Whose side is God on?

Our conversation throbbed with pain because we both knew the details of a budding missionary career that had grievously miscarried. A grim combination of physical, cultural, and emotional difficulties had chewed up the young couple. When they came home, their mangled lives looked like an old car fresh from the recycling yard cruncher.

We didn't talk much about what went wrong, or who was to blame. We thanked God that ever so slowly they were clawing their way out of the pit of despair and showing no signs of lasting bitterness. Then we drifted into some extremely heavy theological traffic, confessing our lack of certainties.

In light of God's universal saving purposes, why do so many missionaries become casualties? Thirty years ago a close friend of mine, whose infectious enthusiasm for a missionary career in Africa had brightened so many people's lives, died of cancer. "God," I prayed, "if missionaries are so desperately needed, why did you take him?"

From my rationalistic perspective, the tragic death of Paul Little in an automobile accident was not the right way to run the universe. He was one of the nation's most effective campus evangelists, teacher and author, and sold out to world missions. What about Chet Bitterman, executed by Colombian terrorists? Or John Speers, gunned down in the Philippines?

All of us could cite similar examples that clog our minds and force us to ask, "God, if you are serious about saving the world, why do you remove some people we think are the best qualified for the job?"

These cases force us to take a deeper look at the theological underpinnings of world missions. We've got to get beyond the immediate, here-and-now, pragmatic approach to world missions. Beyond the engineering model, the big business model, the management by objectives model. Because if we don't, then we will quit and say that world missions is a stupid game.

Unfortunately, heavy theological thinking is perilously absent in much of our current missions enterprise. We have succumbed to obsessive production models. But this approach makes absolutely no sense, because rationally God seems to be his own worst enemy in getting the job done. He takes out some of our best players.

If simply counting missionaries, support dollars, people evangelized, churches planted, patients treated, programs broadcast, and so on, is the goal of world missions, we are on the wrong track. That's not God's goal. He has only one purpose: to glorify himself in the world.

God is not in the assembly line business. The apostle Paul looked around and wanted to consign himself to hell because he couldn't count many Jewish converts. Then he reflected more deeply and realized that it was only because of God's capriciously bestowed mercy and compassion that anyone is saved. I say capriciously, because that's the way it looks to us.

It will always look that way, unless we undergird our minds with God's supremacy, his right to do as he pleases (even to remove missionaries), and his right to bring glory to himself any way he chooses.

Yes, there is a much higher goal for this young couple than achieving a successful career in missions. It is to honor and glorify God with their persistent faith, trust, hope, and obedience. All of us executives, recruiters, fund-raisers, trainers, pastors, and supporters must constantly fight our way through the thickets that pressure us to conform to a rationalistic, humanistic way of looking at world missions. We must come out standing firmly on the higher ground of God's all-wise, all-loving, and self-glorifying purposes.

After Paul resolved his theological conundrum, he did not become a lazy fatalist, forgetting Christ's command to evangelize the world. Rather, with his eyes trained on God's glory, he preached to the point of exhaustion, working tirelessly with all the energy and power that Christ gave him.

Why aren't our teams winning?

If you're between 26 and 44, you're sick and tired of not only being psychoanalyzed, but also marketed, packaged, and dissected. Probably, people under 26 and over 44 are also fed up with all the "baby boomer" stuff. But whatever you make of the stacks of books, articles, and reports about "boomers," they have changed missions.

We are not mere cogs in a machine, the boomer missionaries say, we want to find deeper levels of intimacy, especially with our fellow-workers on the field. Many boomers developed significant partnerships in college, not just with their future wives and husbands, but with people who shared the same values and even the same missionary calling. Out of their profound spiritual desires they conceived missionary church-planting teams.

Meanwhile, sending agencies were taking heat for what appeared to be their sacrificing of lonely couples in desolate, unresponsive places, so they, too, were looking for missionary teams, but for pragmatic reasons: to stave off casualities and to get quicker church-planting results. The boomers and the recruiters met each other over pizza one night and the match was done. Church-planting teams flew up and out of New York, Chicago, L.A., Dallas, and Atlanta like colorful balloons released by kids at a Sunday school picnic, and with just as much excitement about anticipated successes. Of course some of those balloons get no further than the nearest tree, others strangle in high tension wires, and a few fizzle out a hundred miles away. Some church-planting teams have suffered similar disasters. It's time to ask why.

For one thing, some of the boomers' hoped-for relational strengths have been gutted, because even highly motivated missionaries on teams can turn on themselves and start picking on each other. Life gets sticky, nerves fray, and the team begins to unravel. In the frontline trenches of spiritual warfare life assumes a less rosy hue than it did back on campus. When babies and bills and furniture and sickness and language study come along, they revert to "wilderness behavior" and lash out at each other and at their Moses.

But, who is Moses on the team? Another reason teams fail is because no one wants to take charge, or because the home office failed to send Moses in time. If he is there, perhaps he needs a Jethro. Teams fall apart because of inept administration.

Before long, both the managers at home and the team on the field begin to look for those new churches that were supposed to be springing up like dandelions in a June lawn. Teams also fail because they lack patience for the long haul—the anticipated successes just aren't there.

Compounding their disappointment is the feeling that the churches in the neighborhood aren't exactly ecstatic either. (Yes, there are some churches that have been around a long time in places where teams want to plant new churches.) Teams flounder in some places because they can't find the right fit. Local pastors get suspicious of these new "players" from the U.S. and wonder why there are so many of them camped on their doorsteps.

It's time to look for some design flaws in our church-planting-by-teams concept. Certainly we must be much less sanguine about our latest missionary "magic bullet," lest we recruit too many teams destined for failure.